GARDENING
in SMALL SPACES

fine
Gardening Design Guides™

GARDENING
in SMALL SPACES

Creative Ideas *from* America's Best Gardeners

The Taunton Press

Other books in the *Fine Gardeing Design Guide* series include: *Creating Beds and Borders,
Designing with Plants, Exploring Garden Style, Landscaping Your Home, Gardening in Containers,*
and *Accent Your Garden.*

Text © 2002 by The Taunton Press, Inc.
All rights reserved.

The Taunton Press, Inc., 63 South Main Street, PO Box 5506, Newtown, CT 06470-5506
e-mail: tp@taunton.com

Distributed by Publishers Group West

T The Taunton Press
Inspiration for hands-on living™

Fine Gardening Design Guides™ is a trademark of The Taunton Press. Inc.,
registered in the U.S. Patent and Trademark Office.

COVER AND INTERIOR DESIGNER: Lori Wendin

LAYOUT ARTIST: Carol Petro

FRONT COVER PHOTOGRAPHER: Nancy Beaubaire, © The Taunton Press, Inc. (large); Steve Silk, © The Taunton
Press, Inc. (inset)

BACK COVER PHOTOGRAPHERS: © Allan Mandell (left); Steve Silk, © The Taunton Press, Inc. (top center);
© Claudia Pilato Maietta (top right); © Jan Moore (bottom left); © Lee Anne White (bottom center);
Nancy Beaubaire, © The Taunton Press, Inc. (bottom right)

LIBRARY OF CONGRESS CATALOGING-IN-PUBLICATION DATA
Gardening in small spaces/the editors of Fine gardening.
    p. cm.–(Fine gardening design guides)
  ISBN 1-56158-580-7
  1. Landscape gardening.   I. Fine gardening.   II. Series.
SB473 .G28895 2002
  635.9'671–dc21

2002007631

Printed in the United States of America
10 9 8 7 6 5 4 3 2 1

*S*pecial thanks to the authors, editors, art directors, copy editors, and other staff members of Fine Gardening *who contributed to the development of the articles in this book.*

Contents

Introduction

Many of us live in urban or suburban areas. The neighborhood is great, the house was affordable, the school system is ideal for our children, but the lot is small and often surrounded by other homes on all sides. Fortunately, small yards and great gardens are not mutually exclusive entities.

Designing small gardens is all about illusion; about making a small space feel larger. These design tricks are based on the same principles used in all garden design—providing visitors with a sense of discovery, creating a sense of depth by choosing plants of various heights and textures, achieving unity through the repetition of color, plants, or building materials, and dividing spaces into rooms for different functions.

Just as important as making the space feel larger is creating privacy. We all need a retreat that makes us feel miles away from the noise and commotion of the outside world—a place where we can enjoy the Sunday morning paper in solitude or in companionship with friends dining al fresco in the evening.

Collected here are articles from some of America's best garden designers who will show you their tricks for creating wonderful gardens out of small spaces. From planning to choosing plants and materials, they'll prove that the smallest town lot can be transformed into a garden paradise.

DESIGN
STRATEGIES

1

DESIGNING A SMALL GARDEN is, in large measure, a matter of manipulation. Without the benefit of a large expanse of space, you need to employ a number of visual tricks that fool the mind into thinking the garden is bigger than it is. It simply may be a matter of pruning trees to create windows through which to glimpse other areas of the garden or dividing a single, open space into smaller "rooms," which actually increases the perception of size rather than decreases it.

Like their larger counterparts, small gardens also need design elements that create a sense of unity within the garden and with the house. The repetition of colors, plants, and building materials helps to achieve this. The examples shown here prove the most successful gardens use multiple devices to achieve their maximum potential.

BETTY RAVENHOLT

grew up in a gardening family and fondly remembers her days spent as the "weeding assistant" in the Tennessee gardens of her mother, aunts, grandmother, and great-grandmother.

Clever Strategies *for Designing* Small Spaces

Add depth to small spaces with color repetition (opposite). The author artfully coordinates the colors in her beds, window boxes, and planted containers.

MY HUSBAND, Reimert, and I garden on a postage-stamp-sized lot. I was hoping for more garden space when we moved to Seattle, but a 100-foot-long sloping embankment bisects our site into two smaller sections. I knew at first sight of that slope that most of my gardening efforts would be confined to the upper lot that surrounds our house.

I started planning, keeping in mind the feeling of "yard" that I had loved during my childhood in the Southeast. The biggest challenge at this new site was how to design an outdoor living area that would seem bigger than it actually was. There was nowhere to go but up, so to create this sense of depth and space, as well as special nook-and-cranny areas for sitting, eating, and relaxing, our only choice was to garden vertically.

VERTICAL STRUCTURES CREATE THE ILLUSION OF SPACE

When we began to plan our new garden, we decided to add a number of structural elements to the landscape to increase its sense of depth. We enclosed our front garden with the vertical palings of a picket fence, buttressed our two front-facing porches with wide and deep brick steps, and built decks at each level of the three-story house. All these elements lead the eye upward and outward, and make the space seem bigger.

Vertical elements like fences, porches, and steps also provide support or platforms for plants and add depth to the garden without taking up much scarce ground space. Terracotta containers arranged on our front steps carry the color combinations in our garden beds right up to our front doors. Arranging groups of pots on several steps increases the

sense of depth, as do the window boxes placed above two relatively shallow perennial beds. Repeating foliage and flower color combinations throughout our beds, pots, and window boxes strengthens the illusion of increased depth.

TRAIN CLIMBING PLANTS TO GROW UP, NOT OUT

Plants trained to grow on vertical structures are good tools to use to create depth in the garden, so we encourage many of our plants to grow up rather than out. We use metal tuteurs and wooden trellises as vertical support structures for our roses and clematis vines. Tuteurs are especially useful in providing structure for some of the David Austin roses in our garden.

We also use existing structures like the skeleton of an old vine maple and a vigorous shrub dogwood (*Cornus alba* 'Argenteomarginata') to support and contain a *Clematis jackmanii* and C. 'Niobe', respectively. We found, however, that fairly ruthless thinning of the dogwood is necessary each spring to be able to see the deep-red 'Niobe' clematis through the dogwood foliage. Without these frameworks, we would not be able to fit these vigorous growers into our limited ground space.

Reimert's experience growing up on a Midwestern farm included growing many vegetables and fruits. In our small space, this posed quite a challenge. So, we included five espaliered fruit trees (two apples, two pears, and a crabapple) in our gardening scheme. These trees grow in a narrow bed against the south side of our house, trained and attached to wires affixed to the wall, with small wooden

Lead the eye upward to points of visual interest. Vertical structures such as fence palings not only support plants in the author's garden but mimic and draw attention to the design of the gables up above.

The author's garden is small—note how the garden bench is visible in all three photos—but the perspective and mood change greatly as one moves upward though this vertical garden. **1.** The garden feels intimate from ground level (above). **2.** The first-story deck (left) provides a bird's-eye view of the seating areas in the garden rooms below. **3.** The second-story deck (right) extends the house into the garden and demonstrates how structure adds depth to this compact space.

Train plants to grow vertically. Espaliered apple and pear trees line the narrow passageway between the author's front garden and her backyard.

CREATE LAYERS AND TEMPER VERTICALITY

While vertical elements are important in disguising our garden's shallow dimensions, we were determined not to create a setting where we felt dwarfed or overwhelmed by height. We keep our gardens tied to the ground and accessible by combining taller plants—a variety of shrubs or perennials that reach up to 4 feet tall—with short- to medium-sized plants (3 feet or less). Stepping down from taller plants to shorter plants not only creates another layer in our garden, but also serves to keep the vertical nature of some of the structural elements in check.

Although the fence palings in the front garden attract the eye and mimic the design of the two front gables, we wanted them to be a backdrop for plants rather than the main garden attraction. Our picket fence not only supports tall plants like *Anchusa* 'Lodden Royalist', *Verbascum chaixii*, and *Rosa* 'Ballerina', but it is also bordered by shorter plants like *Centranthus ruber* and *Nepeta* 'Six Hills Giant'. Plants are allowed to spill through the pickets so that their bulk is not confined within the narrow perimeter of the bed.

blocks placed between the side of the house and the trees' branches to create space for air circulation. The espaliered trees make good use of a narrow space and provide us with edible fruit to boot.

Perhaps the most striking vertical plants in our garden are the four climbing 'America' roses that frame our two front doorways. These hardy and prolific bloomers provide color from May until sometime in December, depending on the weather. Their upright nature adds another layer to the complexity of our garden's design.

USE DEVICES THAT PAUSE THE EYE AND ENLARGE THE SPACE

Experience taught us that barriers of plant material or structure stop the eye and make small areas seem smaller. Our space began to feel larger when we created diversions to delay the eye from reaching the garden's outer limits. Varying foliage texture and color is one device we use. Other elements—

"The espaliered trees make good use of a narrow space and provide us with edible fruit to boot."

such as groups of pots planted with perennials within perennial beds or structures like a birdbath, a small column, or a dripping fountain—provide reasons for looking within a garden and not straight through it.

Having a destination, even in a small area, draws visitors into the garden, around corners, and toward the next view—which increases the sense of space. In our garden, curving paths of stepping-stones, bark mulch, or bluestone set in sand gives a sense that the distance traveled is farther than our small yard actually allows. At the end of each path we've placed either a seat, a small table with chairs, or a cluster of pots. Wherever we go in our garden we can see through the plantings to at least one sitting area that beckons us onward.

CREATE AN INTIMATE SPACE WITH A MIXED TAPESTRY BORDER

Experience taught us another lesson in design: Small spaces do not work well without structure. We had a small-scale, bluestone-floored sitting area at one end of our back garden that was previously set apart by a line of hedge roses. While we liked their informal look and the inviting cottage-garden feel, the roses' prolific growth and

Install eye-catching diversions to keep visitors' attention within the garden's boundaries. Structures such as birdbaths or benches contain wandering eyes.

blowsy habit crowded the area and created visual confusion.

Our daughter Lisa—an avid gardener herself—introduced us to the concept of a "mixed tapestry hedge," made up of slower-growing, midsized, mostly vertical evergreens with contrasting textures and foliage colors.

The plants are placed in such a way that they do not form a solid wall. This relaxed, but structured hedge provides not only a feeling of separateness for this small area, but also a considerable amount of winter interest.

To create our hedge, we chose a number of our favorite evergreens that do well in our

Can't Spread Out? Grow Up!

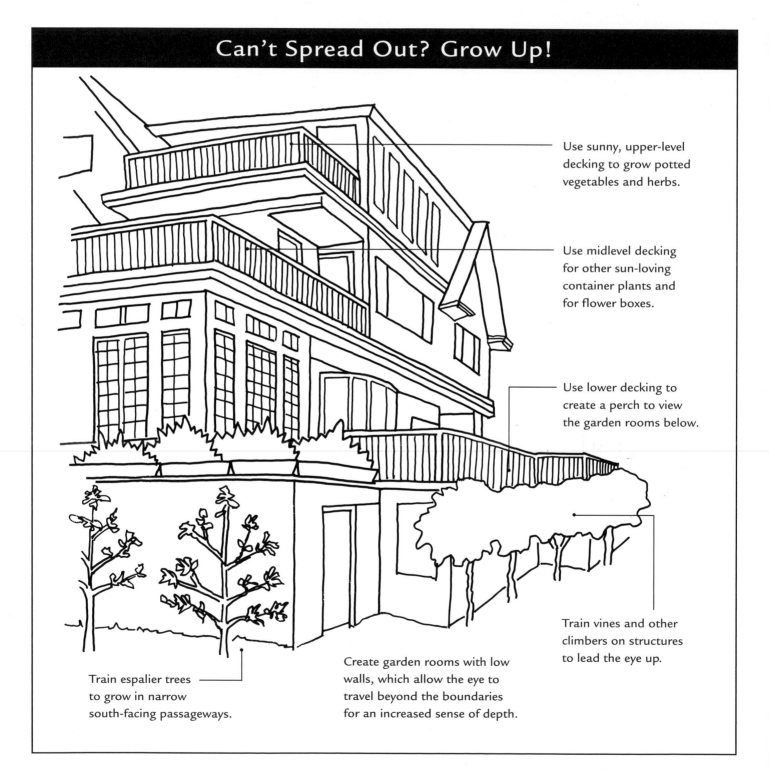

Use sunny, upper-level decking to grow potted vegetables and herbs.

Use midlevel decking for other sun-loving container plants and for flower boxes.

Use lower decking to create a perch to view the garden rooms below.

Train vines and other climbers on structures to lead the eye up.

Train espalier trees to grow in narrow south-facing passageways.

Create garden rooms with low walls, which allow the eye to travel beyond the boundaries for an increased sense of depth.

Plant an open and airy hedge for structure, but not too much. Here, the author combines specimens to create a boundary without blocking views.

area: two Italian cypresses (*Cupressus sempervirens* 'Swane's Gold'), two Chinese junipers (*Juniperus chinensis* 'Blue Point'), a 'Plum Passion' heavenly bamboo (*Nandina domestica* 'Plum Passion'), a 'Spring Bouquet' laurustinus (*Viburnum tinus* 'Spring Bouquet'), a 'Tuscan Blue' rosemary (*Rosmarinus officinalis* 'Tuscan Blue'), an Hinoki false cypress (*Chamaecyparis obtusa* 'Nana Gracilis'), and a potted lavender (*Lavandula* 'Goodwin Creek Gray'). The hedge fills a small area that is 6 feet square. I also chose these plants for the structure and texture they lend to my airy border.

ADD DEPTH TO SMALL SPACES WITH VISUAL DIVERSITY

The most important lesson that we have learned during our years gardening in Seattle is that a garden rich with visual diversity appears to have greater depth. Happily, we can enjoy much of our garden from inside our house. When we look out through window-box flowers and see-through screens of taller plantings to the vertical elements and dense perennial beds, our garden gives us a sense of increased depth and distance even from inside. It's at that moment that we can forget we garden on a postage-stamp-sized lot.

"A garden rich with visual diversity appears to have greater depth."

KEITH DAVITT

is a landscape designer, landscape contractor, and horticulturist. He has spent the last 20 years designing and building landscape projects around the country.

Expansive
Solutions
for Small
Gardens

A garden seems larger if you let it unfold gradually. As you enter the author's garden, you come to the pool and then to the patio beyond.

FOR ME, the intent of landscape design is to create an environment that's both wonderful to see and delightful to experience. This environment is more easily realized where space is plentiful and options are endless. In urban sites, however, space is limited. So how, then, do you create the fun of mystery and discovery, the peace of solitude, the delight of visual intrigue, and the satisfaction of pleasing the senses? How can you divest these little urban yards of that sense of restriction and confinement so many of them seem to convey?

These are the questions I asked myself when I moved to Brooklyn from the rolling fields of North Salem, New York. As a landscape designer coming from the country, these were the challenges I faced.

A WINDING PATH
CREATES SURPRISE

I decided to begin, naturally enough, with my own 32- by 22-foot garden (see Garden 1 on the facing page). Consisting of a central planting area surrounded on three sides by a walkway, the garden seemed static and two-dimensional. Everything was visible at once, and consequently it seemed smaller and more limited—not as interesting and inviting as I wanted it to be.

I thought that if the garden could unfold more gradually, it would seem larger by providing those welcome elements of surprise and discovery that amplify the pleasures of a garden. I also realized that if I put the planting areas on the outer edges, with the living area toward the middle, I could generate more privacy and, at the same time, expand the planting area. This, too, would enhance the sense of spaciousness.

To do this, I built a bluestone path that wanders out from the door to the patio, canopied by two major planting groups on either side. I placed the patio more or less in the center of the yard, planting trees, shrubs, vines, and perennials on all four sides. Adjacent, I built a small fish pond and a stone-faced barbecue.

Now, as you enter the garden area, you get just a glimpse of the pond and a portion of the patio beyond, seen through the leafy overhang of trees and shrubs. It's only as you follow the winding path that the garden opens up. As you push aside the last of the cascading foliage and step forward, you find yourself in a paved clearing, enveloped within leaves and flowers. The impact is palpable.

Once on the patio, the barbecue and dining table suggest their own possibilities, like summer evening parties, candle-lit dinners, and breakfast with the birds. The pool, situated at the patio's edge, offers views of flashing fish and water lilies, as well as the sound of gurgling water. I used larger plants here to screen nearby structures while framing views into the tops of neighboring trees; this, too, seemed to expand the garden. I gave the patio an irregular edge by planting ground covers that obscure the lines, contributing to the sense of graceful ease.

DIVIDING IS MORE
LIKE MULTIPLYING

The next site I designed (see Garden 2 on p. 18) was also afflicted with what seemed like inherent limitations, though different from the ones in my own garden. Exposed as a fish bowl, barren, and narrow, this second lot appeared particularly uninviting and unusable.

To deal with this problem, I created two distinctly separate spaces. Most people tend to think that a small area divided becomes smaller still. Yet if it's done with a sense of proportion and with enough room given to each area, dividing becomes more like multiplying—increasing the perception of space as well as possible experiences.

I made the first space the largest, and ample enough for a variety of outdoor activities, thus eliminating any sense of confinement. The second space, visible through an arbor, invites you onward. When you step into this garden, you can't help but wonder what's back there.

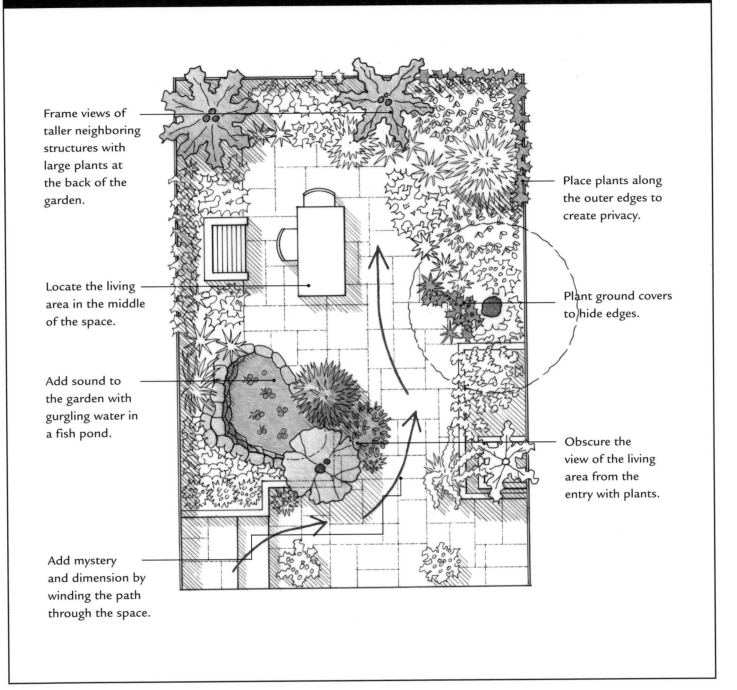

Frame views of taller neighboring structures with large plants at the back of the garden.

Place plants along the outer edges to create privacy.

Locate the living area in the middle of the space.

Plant ground covers to hide edges.

Add sound to the garden with gurgling water in a fish pond.

Obscure the view of the living area from the entry with plants.

Add mystery and dimension by winding the path through the space.

Garden 2: Two Spaces: One Big, One Small

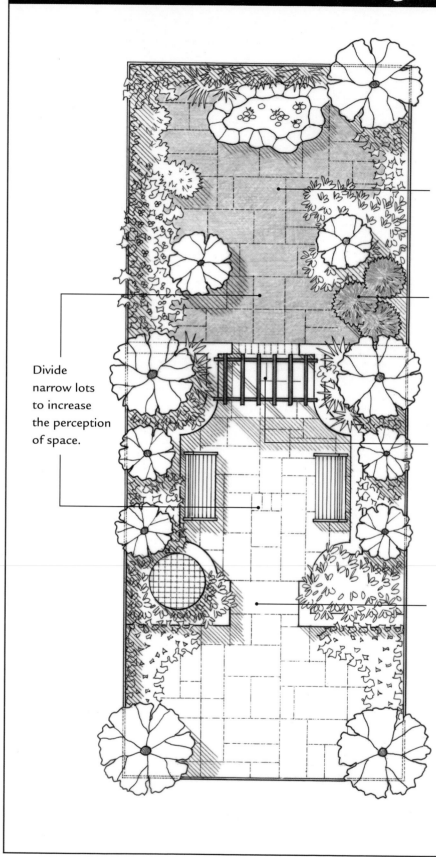

Differentiate the back half of the garden from the front half with a sunken floor.

Add intimacy to the back garden by using taller plants and an informal planting design.

Divide narrow lots to increase the perception of space.

Lead visitors through the space with an arbor that divides and unites the two halves of the garden.

Make the design of the front garden more formal by keeping plantings to a minimum. This area is big enough to hold small gatherings.

To further enhance the sense of separation, I excavated the second area, dropping it several inches below the first. I also gave it an entirely different character from the front garden. The front area is formal in layout; it's symmetrical and made of bluestone with mortared joints and raised brick planters. The rear area, on the other hand, is free-form and informal. It, too, is paved with bluestone, but this time I laid it on top of the soil, with brick randomly worked in. The layout is irregular and the beds are ground level. The built-in sandbox, small water garden, and profusion of wildlife-attracting plants (for the birds, squirrels, butterflies, and dragon-flies) enhance the casual atmosphere.

These garden areas are very different, yet together they create a unity, which is important in maintaining a sense of place. The arbor, for example, both joins the areas and separates them. It helps create a visual barrier while framing a view into the garden and beyond, serving to set each area apart while inviting the visitor from one area into the other.

The use of the same materials—like brick and stone—also helps tie the two areas together, as does the repetition of the more dramatic plants. For example, the eye-catching ornamental grasses and plants with variegated leaves repeat throughout the garden, creating continuity. What was once a site seemingly without possibilities is now a two-room garden offering countless experiences—all achieved through the principle of division.

TERRACING ADDS DIMENSION TO A LONG, NARROW SPACE

Dividing by three works, too. Another site I designed (see Garden 3 on p. 20) was about 80 by 20 feet—quite large by urban standards,

yet it seemed tiny and inaccessible. Part of the problem, as is often the case with small properties, was in the unfortunate division of space. Two poorly placed cedar trees created a cramped patio area near the house entry, while an overgrown crabapple tree crowded out the rear portion of the garden.

The first thing I did was get rid of these trees. But even when they were gone, the site still seemed too confining. This was due to the extreme narrowness of the lot in contrast to the height of the building. To reduce the unfortunate length-to-width ratio, I divided

The use of the same materials and the repetition of plants creates unity within a garden. Here, the author used brick and stonework, as well as ornamental grasses, to tie two distinct areas together.

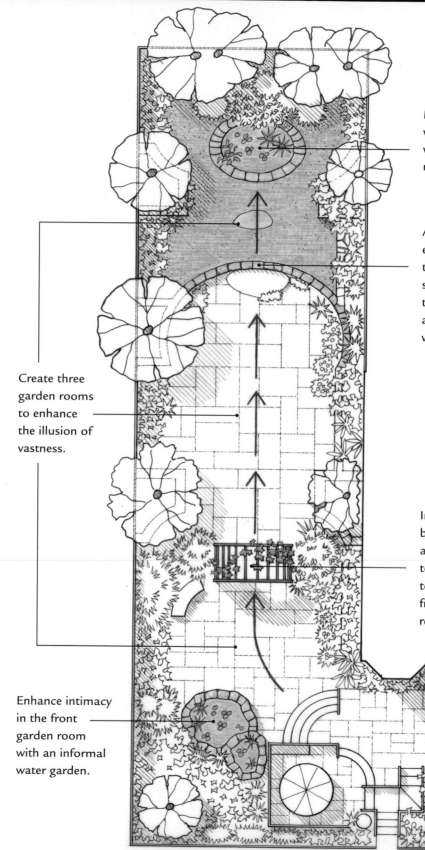

Mask street noises with gurgling water in the raised garden.

Accent the higher elevation of the third room and separate it from the second with a low retaining wall.

Create three garden rooms to enhance the illusion of vastness.

Install an arbor between the first and second rooms to signal a change to the visitor and frame a view to the rear of the garden.

Enhance intimacy in the front garden room with an informal water garden.

Terracing is a great way to add dimension to your garden, as well as to separate space. Here, a low stone wall leads the eye to the water garden.

this lot into three separate areas. Because the yard was very long and easily supported three areas, creating three rooms would enhance interest and possibility. Moreover, because the yard rose noticeably toward the farthest area in the lawn (where the semiformal water garden is now located), terracing was a natural treatment here.

The area closest to the house features a redwood deck that flows easily down to an intimate patio that's accented by an informal water garden and graceful plantings. I separated this first space from the second one by installing a wide arbor that permits an easy view into the second and third garden areas.

The second area is the largest and adds considerably to the yard's overall sense of spaciousness. You move from an intimate yet ample deck and patio area into a more roomy area that offers a view into still another chamber of the garden. This experience of motion, of expansion through space, creates the illusion of vastness.

The third area of this garden is elevated and separated from the second area by a low stone wall. Proportion here is important. If

An entry arch separates the first garden from the second and frames a view of the second and third garden areas.

too tall, the wall would have the effect of a barrier, inhibiting forward motion; if too low, it would seem foolish and unnecessary. As it is, the wall lifts the eye, carrying your vision into some remote point undeterminable because of the abundant plantings at the rear of the garden.

The semiformal water garden in the third area serves several functions. An ornament in itself, the water garden sits like a jewel in its verdant surroundings, providing both visual and auditory interest, as well as masking street noises. The water garden also serves as a focal point, starting from the very front of the garden where it draws your attention from the deck through the entire expanse of the landscape.

Though filled with diversity, these three garden spaces are welded into one environment by two primary elements—the use of stone throughout and the repetition of form. Stone planters on the left balance the dry-laid stone wall on the right and rear, while the curve of the arbor, the rear retaining wall, the planters, and the water garden help integrate each area into a consistent whole.

CURVES AND DIAGONALS ADD INTRIGUE

Creating divisions and providing mystery are not the only ways to enlarge small places. Working with line is also important. Because the shortest distance between two points is a straight line—visually as well as physically—

Using curved lines in garden design keeps you from seeing everything at once. This curved wall not only supports the raised beds and the water garden, but it does away with the static, linear quality found in many small spaces.

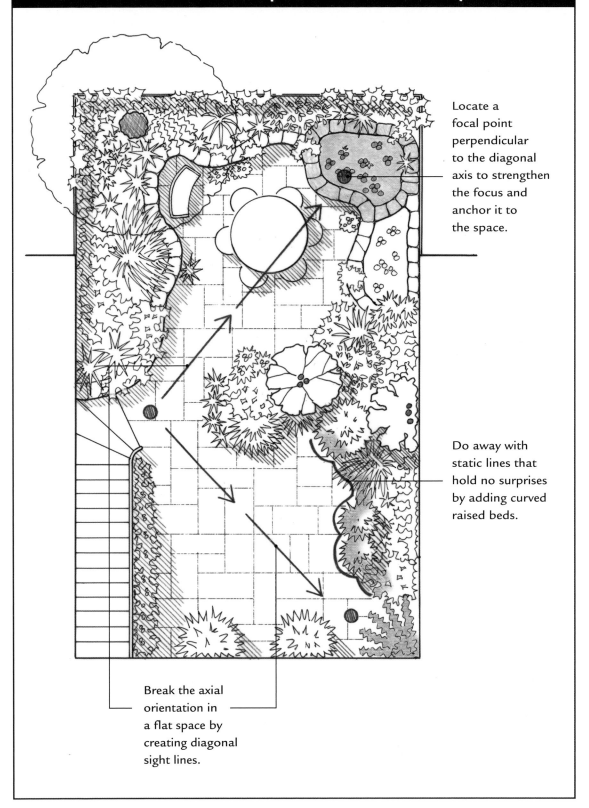

Locate a focal point perpendicular to the diagonal axis to strengthen the focus and anchor it to the space.

Do away with static lines that hold no surprises by adding curved raised beds.

Break the axial orientation in a flat space by creating diagonal sight lines.

"I am now convinced that there is no site—no matter how small—that cannot be effectively transformed."

when everything in a small space is linear, we see everything at once. Our eyes don't traverse the length of the line, but go immediately to the end, taking no joy in the journey. The space seems to shrink as we instantly see the whole garden at once.

Consider, for example, this next urban landscape (see Garden 4 on p. 23). It was a dark, flat, two-dimensional rectangle, utterly without interest. By building a curved wall that supports the raised beds and the water garden, I succeeded in doing away with that static, linear quality. Now, our attention is first swept along this curve but then leaps away at various points to different views the garden offers.

Diagonal lines can be used for the same effect. For example, a patio laid diagonally to the length-width axis of a given area will pleasantly break up our customary axial orientation and help convey a greater sense of space. When using diagonals, I try to incorporate other elements within that orientation. I might, for instance, allow a portion of a retaining wall to sweep out and follow the diagonal lines of the patio for some distance. Or I may place an arbor perpendicular to the diagonal axis, thereby strengthening the diagonal focus and anchoring it within the total space.

SPECIAL ELEMENTS PIQUE INTEREST

The use of detail is valuable in adding depth and dimension to small places and can be included in a variety of ways. Any element that enhances our senses has the effect of expanding and prolonging our garden experience.

Water gardens are ideal for this, and I've made it a point to include them in many of my gardens. Consider the delightful sound of cascading water, reflections on a placid pool, the colors and motion of swimming fish, and day- and night-blooming water lilies. What other elements offer so much in so little space?

Except, of course, plants. Combined well, planting groups can add vitality and liveliness to a landscape. What's important here is that the plants have a perceivable relationship to one another, that they interact, visually, through the principles of harmony and contrast in respect to their forms and textures.

I was concerned when I first encountered these urban sites and the problems that came with them. I was worried I wouldn't be able to create beautiful gardens. After several years of finding solutions satisfying to both my clients and me, I am now convinced that there is no site—no matter how small—that cannot be effectively transformed. If you have a tiny would-be garden, chances are it only awaits the application of a few of these principles before it, too, becomes a garden that gives you lasting pleasure.

ELLEN FISHER

is a certified landscape designer in Nashua, New Hampshire. She is currently working in public land management and conservation.

Reshaping *Small* Spaces

The circle garden was one of three garden rooms created from a narrow corridor.

ROSEMARY MACK loved to hear the stories about Daisy Goldsmith. For 40 summers, Daisy had filled her yard with flowers and the neighborhood children with homemade cookies. She always walked around barefoot, and she laughingly said that she never cleaned her house in the summer because she would rather be outside, tending her plants. But now that Rosemary and her husband were living in Daisy's trim Cape Cod house, they could find little evidence of her charming, flower-filled garden.

After Daisy moved out of the house in 1984, subsequent owners changed the yard considerably—eliminating the flower and vegetable beds, adding conventional foundation plantings, and "neatening up" the yard. Just four years later, only a few small trees, a lilac, some mountain laurel, two gigantic blueberry bushes, and a handful of

Canterbury bells and foxgloves remind Rosemary of Daisy, who once filled the yard with flowers.

THE CHALLENGE: A NARROW, CORRIDOR SPACE

Rosemary and her husband live on a small city lot—less than 10,000 square feet. The backyard was a long, narrow lawn enclosed by a privacy fence. At 30 feet deep and 100 feet wide, I consider it a corridor space. Corridors don't feel like rooms, or places to relax in. Instead, they feel more like hallways, or places to move through.

In one corner, she built a few raised garden beds, but she wasn't happy with them. Shade from the fence and overhanging trees limited what she could grow. Even though there were several beautiful garden features, she told me that nothing about her yard "felt right."

Rosemary said that she wanted to do more gardening, and she gave me an ambitious list of plants she wanted to grow; most of them were sun lovers. She wanted her garden to be a beautiful place, where she could relax in her hand-built Adirondack chairs and settee. As we walked around, she lovingly showed me Daisy's plants and asked me to preserve them in the new plan.

THE SOLUTION: CREATE INDIVIDUAL GARDEN ROOMS

The back of the house, with its pleasant, airy porch, roughly faces south, so it was the area with the most sun on the property. The light was best close to the house, however, not deep in the corners where Rosemary had placed her raised garden beds. I knew that most of the sun-loving plants Rosemary longed to grow should be located just outside the back door.

tough perennials were all that remained scattered about the yard as a reminder of Daisy's presence.

Although Rosemary never set out to re-create Daisy's garden, she did want a place to grow a few flowers for cutting and some herbs for cooking. Rosemary had little gardening experience when she called to consult me about the yard, but through the years, she has developed into a sophisticated, yet playful, gardener. Together, I believe we have created a place that Daisy would love. I designed the plan; Rosemary installed it, tends the gardens, and sees it through annual changes.

To eliminate the corridor feel and make the yard more inviting, I subdivided the backyard into three rooms, each one about 30 feet square, and assigned each room a function. The yard is small, but this made it seem larger.

A sitting room

The southeast corner became the sitting area and the only area that still has lawn. It was already framed by Daisy's mountain laurel, lilac, and dogwood, so it easily became a lovely setting for lawn furniture.

Originally, there was a bulkhead jutting out into this space and a small patio between it and the house. We eliminated the patio and blended the bulkhead into the mixed border, thus disguising its intrusive shape while preserving access to the basement.

A circle garden

The sunny center became a circle garden—the most formal space—to be used for ornamental gardening. The central circle is located directly in line with the back door of the porch.

The sitting room invites visitors to rest and enjoy the views of the garden.

The circular garden, located just outside the back door, is filled with Rosemary's favorite flowers and edged in brick.

When Rosemary steps out the door, she's right in the middle of her garden. Almost all the beds in the circle garden are in full sun, providing a highly visible place for Rosemary's favorite flowers. She edged the beds with brick and settled on pea gravel for the paths.

I love Rosemary's creative planting schemes. One year, in the center circle, she made a "lemon bed" with lemon thyme, lemon gem marigolds, lemon verbena, lemon balm, lemon-scented geraniums, and yellow nasturtiums. In another area, she planted precious metals: gold and silver thyme, bronze fennel, and diamond gem lettuce.

These whimsical combinations have been very successful, and once I got the puns, they were even more enjoyable.

Vegetable and nursery beds

The southwest corner, where Rosemary had her original beds, became a vegetable garden and nursery bed. I moved the beds further into the sun and reshaped them to fill the space. This area is set off from the rest of the backyard by a 4-foot-tall picket fence with a gate. The gate is an eye-catching feature that can be seen from any of the backyard spaces. Daisy's two blueberry bushes overhang the fence, giving it a long-established look.

Rosemary moved three of Daisy's plants to this area, creating one of her favorite combinations. When the orange flame azalea blooms behind a bed of reddish-orange oriental poppies and deep-yellow bearded irises, their brilliant color can be seen through the veil of the fence from all over the backyard.

The vegetable garden is filled with lettuces, squash, beets, peppers, eggplants, herbs, and a few tomatoes. Rosemary uses her nursery beds as a temporary home for annuals and perennials she grows each year from seed.

PATHWAYS CONNECT THE GARDEN ROOMS

A 4-foot-wide path parallels the back of the house and joins all three garden rooms. It is wide enough for a wheelbarrow to pass through. The other paths in this garden are 3 feet wide to allow more space for planting.

A picket fence defines the vegetable garden. Nursery beds allow the homeowner to grow annuals and perennials from seed before transplanting them to other areas of the garden.

In the vegetable and nursery area, a walkway connects the front and back yards, and provides access to the utility area. Compost bins, tool and equipment storage, and a potting bench are located here, out of sight, but accessible.

A FUNCTIONAL DESIGN SETS THE STAGE FOR CREATIVITY

Rosemary never met Daisy, but she feels a connection to her. Hailey and Elise, daughters of a man who was one of Daisy's young friends, love to visit. To their delight,

A Backyard Transformation

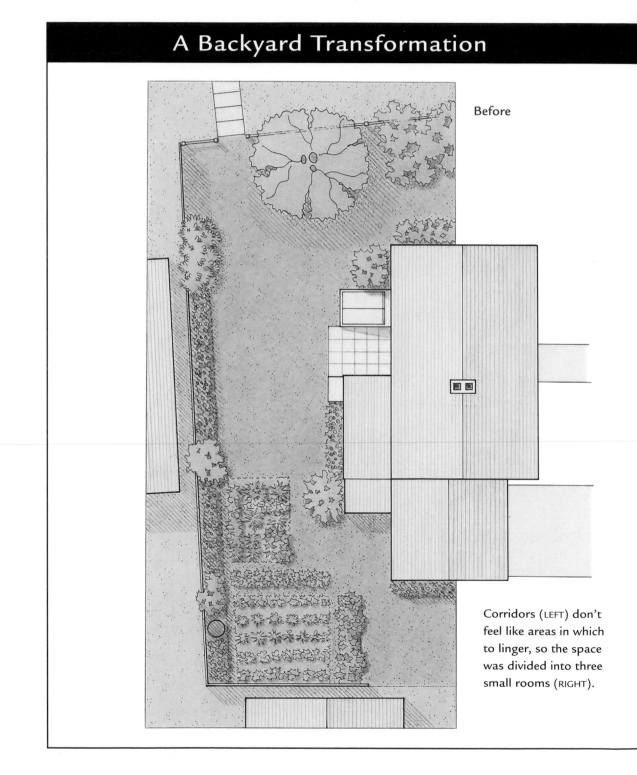

Before

Corridors (LEFT) don't feel like areas in which to linger, so the space was divided into three small rooms (RIGHT).

Rosemary planted a small children's garden with plants to touch and smell, a child-sized wheelbarrow and gardening tools, and a teepee covered with canary creeper vine.

Within the framework of an organized and functional garden design, Rosemary is able to do lots of gardening on her small property. Her imagination and experimentation within the design are what make her garden special. It is the rich, but not overdone, complexity that makes her small garden seem quite large. The neighbors tell Rosemary that she is gardening "just like Daisy."

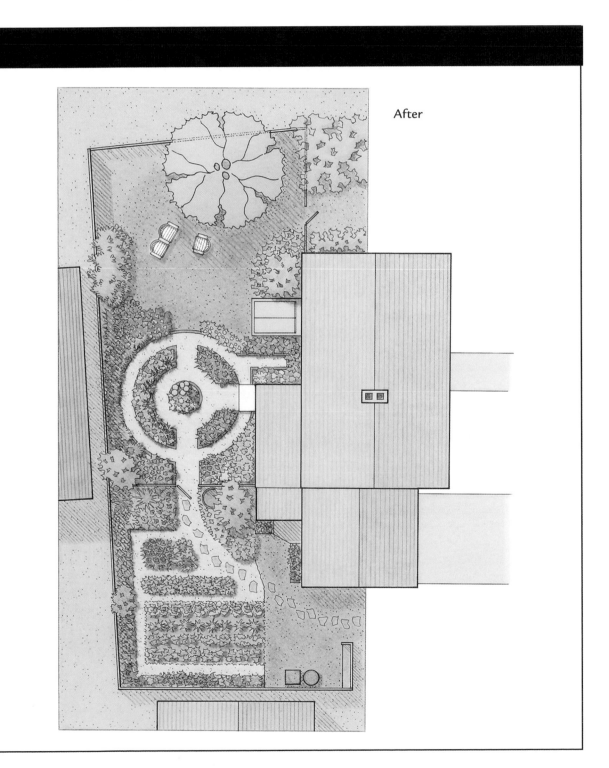

After

Pillars frame the view from the sitting area, revealing the back of the house, brick paving, and a small patch of lawn. (Photo taken at E on site plan.)

ORENE HORTON

teaches, consults, and writes about gardening in Columbia, South Carolina.

Garden Rooms

WHEN WE BOUGHT our house in 1978, the state of the "garden" could have been viewed as a huge problem or a grand opportunity. The backyard was little more than a dirt parking lot; wonderful old camellias overwhelmed the house and blocked many windows; and the front yard was only a boring stretch of grass from foundation planting to curb. Five 60-year-old trees cast dense shade over the long, narrow lot.

A landscape architect helped us to see that dividing the yard into garden rooms—distinctive, separate areas— could give us the illusion of more space. As we've added the plants of our choice over the years, that original organization has served us well.

A FEELING OF PRIVACY

When we started the garden, we needed privacy. For one thing, neighbors are close to our 60-by-150 ft. property here in Columbia, South Carolina. What's more, before we could add plants, we had to remove some. To open up some of the space, we sacrificed a deodar cedar in front and two of three huge pecan trees in back.

Behind the house, we saved a hedge of old camellias on the back property line, and planted clematis (the evergreen *Clematis armandii*) to cover one neighbor's chain-link fence. On the west side of the property we erected a brick wall.

To give a sense of enclosure to the front garden without walling it in, we replaced the old, straight driveway with one that curves inward, allowing room for a shrub border on the property line, echoed by a similar bed on the other side. In the high shade of a Darlington oak, salvaged camellias and azaleas, plus gardenia, daphne, rhododendron, and several kinds of hydrangeas grow happily, underplanted with spring-flowering bulbs. To make the front garden seem wider, we tore out the straight-up-the-middle path to the front door and laid a brick path that curves across the width of the yard and leads through a gate to a side garden and path to the backyard.

As my interest in plants grew, I couldn't help eyeing all that grass in the front yard. I have nothing against grass, but one needs only enough perfectly maintained turf to serve as a foil for other plantings. I also wanted to finish enclosing the property by creating a courtyard effect out front, so about four years ago I designed a new bed along the street (top photo, facing page). I installed a wrought iron fence and planted a narrow bed on the street side with dwarf Japanese Helleri holly, variegated aspidistra, spring bulbs, and hostas. On the house side, I planted a deep, curving bed. Edged with a brick mowing strip, it is anchored by boxwoods and two small trees—a Japanese maple with variegated green-and-cream leaves edged with pink in the spring (*Acer palmatum*

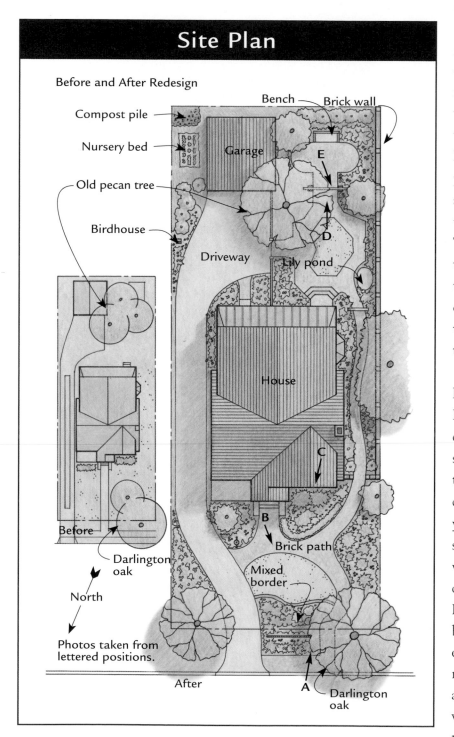

Site Plan

Before and After Redesign

- Compost pile
- Nursery bed
- Old pecan tree
- Birdhouse
- Garage
- Driveway
- Bench
- Brick wall
- E
- D
- Lily pond
- House
- C
- B
- Brick path
- Mixed border
- A
- Darlington oak
- Before
- Darlington oak
- North
- Photos taken from lettered positions.
- After

'Butterfly') and a double-flowered star magnolia (*Magnolia stellata* 'Royal Star'). Deciduous shrubs, perennials, annuals, and bulbs provide seasonal changes of color. The view from all our front windows is now much more private and interesting.

A SUITE OF ROOMS

The backyard is divided into four different garden rooms. The first is our outdoor entertainment area, a spot of lawn bordered by brick paths that widen in several places to accommodate tables and chairs. Flower beds line the perimeter. The remaining pecan tree, limbed up high, shades this area. A small pool and fountain tucked into a corner greet you with the sound of water as you enter on the path from the front yard.

A second garden room can be glimpsed through an opening in a hedge that is framed by two brick columns topped with a cypress

A fence, mixed border, and curving brick path make the author's front yard a garden room. (Photo taken at A on site plan.)

A pair of brick pillars defines the entry to a small sitting area in the back of the property, the section that once housed the children's play equipment. (Photo taken at D on site plan.)

Containers of colorful annuals and perennials brighten the back steps of the house and turn pavement into planting space.

beam. A bench in the background beckons. I designed this area as a sitting garden to replace what used to be our children's play area. It is planted mainly with whites and cool pastels—white tulips in spring, white roses in summer underplanted with lamb's ears and rue, and sweet autumn clematis that scrambles over the back wall and shrubs to bloom in a fragrant froth of tiny, white flowers in late summer. A hedge of laurustinus viburnum (*Viburnum tinus*), clipped to the same height as the 8-ft. columns, encloses this garden. The back wall is formed by a line of old *Camellia sasanqua*, whose fragrant, pale pink blossoms invite you to sit and enjoy the welcome cool weather in fall.

My husband, Tate, built the brick columns that frame the entrance to this garden as well as the brick edging around the planting beds. He probably regrets having ever signed up for the bricklaying course at the local technical college, because I always have a new project to occupy his weekends. After years of dreaming, this spring we finally added two feet to the height of our 5-foot garden wall, but Tate was spared—we contracted out that project. At last I have a wall high enough to support large, climbing roses mingled with clematis. I can hardly wait for them to grow!

An elegant, white birdhouse across the driveway, glimpsed through a honeysuckle-covered arbor in a picket fence, draws you through the gate to a third small room. Although this is the service area, there are beds on either side of the driveway planted for a cottage-garden effect with roses, daisies, phlox, coneflowers, and a couple of clumps of ornamental grasses. By the back door, I grow a few herbs in a small, sunny bed. Finally, I have a raised bed for starting seeds and cuttings, and a compost pile in one last small, concealed area between the garage and the property line.

Containers allow me to grow still more plants. A large collection of pots decorates my back steps. Smaller pots contain sedums, which thrive in spite of our hot summers. I fill larger pots with cascading blue plumbago, pale pink and white fibrous begonias, variegated ivies, white *Zinnia linearis*, and annual vinca (*Catharanthus roseus*). In the fall I plant blue and white pansies over tulip bulbs. Large, painted whiskey barrels by the picket fence gate contain impatiens and variegated ivy in summer and pansies and tulips in spring.

The window boxes outside our breakfast room are filled with similar combinations.

GIVING A COLLECTION UNITY

An avid collector with a small garden must deal with the problem of how to work in a lot of different plants and still maintain a cohesive design. I have found that it fosters unity to repeat certain key plants and building elements throughout the garden. For example, boxwood (the small evergreen shrub) does well for me. I have used it as background material in front and back, in planters and as a featured plant in several mixed borders. Camellias and Indica azaleas are repeated in several locations. And ivy is everywhere. It clothes the walls on at least three sides of the house and fills a bed under a white crape myrtle at the front entrance. Hydrangeas, hostas, ferns, and nandina (heavenly bamboo)

The remaining lawn is small, yet big enough to serve as a cool foil for the brick and for the more colorful flowers. (Photo taken at C on site plan.)

also repeat. Tender evergreen shrubs, vines, and perennials that do well here—fatsia, pittosporum, aspidistra, Confederate jasmine, and holly ferns—give a sense of structure in winter as well as a feeling of continuity.

I also repeat building materials: brick for paving, walls, columns, and bed edgings; wrought iron for fences, porch railings, and gates. The white of the house trim repeats in the picket fence, arbor, garage, and birdhouse. Charleston green is used on all the ironwork (gates, porch railings, dining furniture, rose arch) and many painted, concrete pots. I never add anything new to the design without first considering how compatible it will be with what is already here. With the strong sense of order afforded by all these elements, plantings can be varied and exuberant and still seem perfectly composed.

MIXING PLANTS, MATCHING CONDITIONS

Because I have a small lot with two large trees, I've had to adapt my plantings to shade. It's hard to grow grass under large trees, and a sandy soil and a hot climate compound the problem. Fortunately, there are many plants that will thrive in shade if given good soil and

Shrubs beneath an outstretched oak enclose the front yard and screen the view of the street. (Photo taken at B on site plan.)

Hydrangea macrophylla 'Mariesii' brightens a dark front corner under a mature oak. The white-edged leaves put the shrub among author Horton's favorite variegated plants.

enough water. Liberal additions of compost help with the first requirement, and a sprinkler system helps me keep up with water demands. Under my large oak tree, for example, I enriched the soil with lots of compost and created a mixed planting of oakleaf hydrangeas, holly ferns, hostas, wild ginger, hellebores, variegated Solomon's seal, rohdea, Japanese painted fern, and even some cyclamen and primroses, all bordered by variegated liriope. This bed requires no more water or care than grass does, but it has interesting textures and color all year.

The last and most enjoyable part of designing a garden is choosing plants. Over the years I've kept careful records of what does well in my garden and when different plants bloom. My garden diary has helped me to plan for complementary seasonal displays and to avoid repeating mistakes. No more late red camellias blooming beside magenta azaleas! I enjoy designing beds for interesting combinations of foliage and texture, such as hostas with ferns and aspidistra, and I enjoy combining the colors of foliage and flowers to good effect. I like the purple-leaved barberry (*Berberis thunbergii* 'Rose Glow') underplanted with the chartreuse-leaved form of creeping

"My garden diary has helped me to plan for complementary seasonal displays and to avoid repeating mistakes."

"I'm mad about variegated plants. They are so effective in shade, where they seem to pull in a touch of sunlight."

Jenny (*Lysimachia nummularia* 'Aurea') and the hot pink aster 'Alma Potschke'.

I'm mad about variegated plants. They are so effective in shade, where they seem to pull in a touch of sunlight. I especially love the variegated form of *Hydrangea macrophylla* 'Mariesii' with its delicate blue, lacecap blooms. For containers, nothing makes a better underpinning than a variegated ivy such as 'Glacier', which combines well with almost any color.

FLOWERS YEAR-ROUND

The challenge as well as the joy of gardening in South Carolina's Midlands is to have something in bloom every month of the year. While we are famous for our glorious spring display of dogwoods and azaleas, there are too many other possibilities to allow oneself to succumb to the springtime craze by planting even more of these plants. I enjoy the flowers of Lenten roses (or hellebores) and the fragrant shrub *Daphne odora* in January and February, and the flowers of *Camellia sasanqua* from October through December. The beautiful, red-and-white-striped blooms of a tree form *Camellia japonica* present their display at my dining room window all through the Christmas holidays. The sweet scent of tea olive (*Osmanthus fragrans*) fills the air many times during the year, and the

autumn-flowering cherry (*Prunus subhirtella* 'Autumnalis') blooms practically all winter before its spring show.

Spring comes very early here, and perennials described as midsummer bloomers are often in bloom in May or early June, along with all the roses and the remaining cool-season annuals. It's quite a feast while it lasts, but there are many long, hot days of summer and early fall ahead. Some gardeners opt for all green and retire to air conditioning, but in most of the United States, many long-lasting perennials and repeat-blooming garden roses will carry the colors on until autumn.

Over time, I have discovered plants that perform during our summers. Native and improved forms of the perennial verbenas do well here in containers or in the border. Salvias have proved to be a wonderful genus for summer-long interest. They provide many shades of blue, a color that is so necessary for most color schemes. I have several hard-working favorites, among them the intensely blue *Salvia guaranitica*, which continues from summer until frost. It combines beautifully with the delicate white blooms of *Asteromoea mongolica* and any color of rose. *Salvia* × 'Indigo Spires' is an imposing 4-by- 4-foot specimen whose dusky blue blooms are constantly covered with bees. *Salvia forskhalii* repeatedly sends up spikes of white-lipped, lavender flowers among the blooms of 'Buff Beauty' rose. Finally, the

Roses for Warm Climates

I must have roses. But in our climate, finding roses that lose their leaves to the fungal disease black spot is a challenge. I've thrown away many more than I've kept, but I'm discovering the ones that can take the heat, hold their leaves, keep on blooming and grow with other plants. The pink blooms of 'Carefree Beauty' repeat many times in a season, and this shrub really does live up to its name. Two yellow floribundas, 'All Gold' and 'Sun Flare', are very disease-resistant, as are 'The Fairy', a pink polyantha, 'Little White Pet', another polyantha, and 'Nearly Wild', a single, pink floribunda. 'Dortmund', a red climber, has been most successful. Old garden roses offer more possibilities. The delicate, pink blooms of 'Nastarana', a Noisette, fill the sitting garden with their perfume, and the old climbing tea rose 'Sombreuil' greets me with wonderful fragrance and a showering of pale petals on a path.

show is joined in August by the gray-leaved, purple-flowered *Salvia leucantha*, which also continues until frost.

Summer-blooming shrubs and ornamental grasses offer still more possibilities. I adore all the hydrangeas with their extravagant flowers that gradually fade and soften over time. Next I love *Buddleia davidii* in white, pink, wine, and purple forms, blooming tirelessly from summer until frost if it is kept deadheaded. The ornamental grasses also contribute grace and form to the perennial borders, and bloom at a most welcome time. I favor *Miscanthus sinensis* 'Morning Light' and *M. sinensis* 'Gracillimus', for their slender, graceful foliage.

It's unwise to become too sentimental about plants. I am still looking for more roses, though I will have to get rid of one to add another. Nothing—well, almost nothing—is sacred. So far, only the oak tree and one pecan tree have escaped my shovel-and-wheelbarrow brigade. My husband says he's sure he's moved every shrub in our garden at least three times. By now I have my plants so well trained that they practically leap out of the ground when the wheelbarrow rolls by. If a plant doesn't work in a combination or if it looks unhappy, I may move it to a more promising spot or I may give it away. But I won't hesitate to compost it if it doesn't meet expectations. Life is too short, and there are too many wonderful plants waiting to be tried.

ELEANOR THIENES

is a garden designer who looks outward from the windows in her garden overlooking Lake Washington in Seattle, Washington.

Pruning *for a* View

Vigilant pruning by the author has turned shrubs into ground cover creating an unusual carpet of flowering azaleas and rhododendrons. (Photo taken at A on site plan.)

MY COLLECTION of plants keeps growing. The space I have to plant them in doesn't. So it's an ever-changing challenge to fit them into the front and side yards of my steeply sloped, 100-by-138-foot corner lot. To sculpt the garden and keep making more room, I set off plants with short, dense shapes against plants with tall forms, and I keep them all trimmed so that they share the limited space gracefully.

Judicious pruning is the secret. Twenty years ago my husband, Paul, and I covered our sloping lot with rhodo-dendrons, azaleas, small ornamental deciduous and coniferous trees, flowering perennials, native plants, and ground covers. The colors and textures of the plants combined to form a low-growing, colorful tapestry. We enjoyed the effect, and we didn't want to lose it. But to preserve the garden's appearance, I knew that I would

"I aim to prune up to a third of a shrub or tree each year in order to maintain its size and shape."

need to maintain the size and shape of its plants. I decided to get some pruning shears.

LEARNING TO PRUNE

I learned to prune through study and practice. Two books were especially helpful— *Pruning Techniques* (Brooklyn Botanic Garden Plants & Gardens Handbook), which

describes current pruning methods, and *The Complete Shade Gardener,* by George Schenk (Houghton Mifflin Co.), which includes an inspirational chapter entitled "Creative Pruning."

To develop our hands-on skills, Paul and I attended pruning workshops at a local arboretum. I improved my pruning by using my clippers often and appropriately. Now I carry them with me each time I go to the garden so that I can make cuts to shape plants whenever there's a need, and I always disinfect my pruning tools with methyl alcohol between cuts to prevent spreading disease.

Site Plan

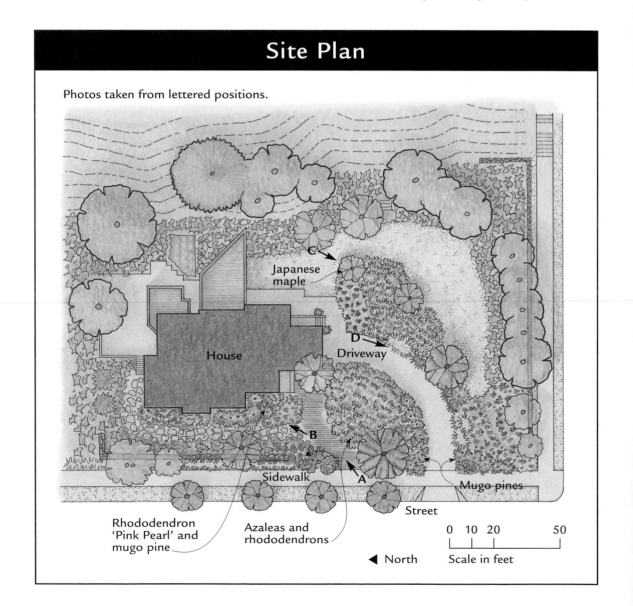

Photos taken from lettered positions.

Japanese maple

House

Driveway

Sidewalk

Mugo pines

Street

Rhododendron 'Pink Pearl' and mugo pine

Azaleas and rhododendrons

0 10 20   50

◀ North   Scale in feet

When pruning, I warm up by clipping small twigs and small branches, and then work up to pruning sizable branches. I aim to prune up to a third of a shrub or tree each year in order to maintain its size and shape. Pruning more than a third of a plant is not good practice because it can encourage weak, limp growth, called rank growth. I also deadhead flowering plants and keep rhododendrons compact by pulling off the leaf bud at the tip of each branch.

KEEP SHRUBS COMPACT

When pruning shrubs to keep them low-growing and compact, I remove branches that grow straight up and leave those that arch gracefully downward or creep along the ground. Trimmed this way, the azalea 'Shirley Jean North' forms a stunning ground cover that smothers the slope with salmon-colored flowers each May. I pruned a group of coral-and-white-flowered satsuki azaleas into a low, undulating drift beneath the 7-foot-tall, pale-yellow-flowered rhododendron 'Carolyn Grace'. This rhododendron, which I pruned to be quite open, gives a feeling of height to the drift without casting too much shade on the azaleas growing beneath it.

Paul softened the edges of the driveway by shaping groups of mugo pine trees (*Pinus mugo pumilo*) that grow along it into low drifts. To promote natural-looking growth, he reaches inside the shrubs to cut back individual branches that grow too tall.

PRUNE TREES TO CREATE WINDOWS

I like to look through deciduous trees to other parts of the garden, so I prune them by removing branches to form openings that I

(LEFT) Brilliant flowers of rhododendron 'Pink Pearl' shine through openings pruned into a 50-year-old mugo pine. (Photo taken at B on site plan.)

(BELOW) A maple adds height to a bed containing fountain grass, pruned rhododendrons, bristlecone pine, an orange-foliated sourwood tree, and red Japanese blood grass. (Photo taken at D on site plan.)

Pruning a Tree to Create Windows

1. Don't injure protective tissue. Preserve the protective tissue at the base of a branch by sawing downward and outward, almost all the way through a branch.

2. Prevent bark from ripping at the base of a branch by keeping the branch steady and completing the cut by sawing upward from the base.

After studying the form of a young Japanese maple (*Acer palmatum* 'Scolopendriifolium') growing near my house, I felt that it needed to be pruned. I couldn't see the inner structure of the tree as I wanted to, I thought it was too tall, and it blocked my view of the garden.

To remedy the situation, I decided to remove selected branches to create an opening, or window, in the canopy of the tree so that I could look through it and enjoy my garden. Trees with windows retain enough foliage to provide a sense of privacy, but the openings allow glimpses of the view beyond them.

I chose which branches to remove as I worked, studying the tree's appearance after each cut. First, I clipped out small, crossed branches at the top of the tree and worked downward. Then I opened up a window in the tree by sawing out a large

interior branch, removing it in two manageable sections, again working from the top down (see the photos above). When removing branches from the trunk, I cut a short distance away from the trunk, sawing downward from the top of the branch and slightly outward as I approached the branch's base. I left the rounded mound at the base of the branch, or collar, attached to the tree (see the top center photo), because removing or damaging a collar can prevent the formation of healing tissue, or callus, and invite disease.

After I had removed the lowest portion of the big branch, the pruned tree looked airier and more sculptural. The spacing of the remaining branches pleased my eye, and I could easily see through the window I had opened to the garden beyond it (see the photo at right).

3. Open up space, or a "window," in the center of the tree by removing a large lower limb.

4. Glimpses of the garden show through a "window" created by pruning this Japanese maple. (Photo taken at C on site plan.)

call "windows." I especially like to open windows in trees that grow in front of the house, because the filminess of the pruned foliage gives me a feeling of privacy, but at the same time I can see through it to the world beyond.

Paul prunes evergreen trees by clipping them to create tall, open shapes. He trained three large evergreens that were blocking the front door into spare shapes, each about 7 or 8 feet tall.

To create open-looking evergreen trees, Paul removes limbs that cross and branches that grow downward, and keeps the branches that grow upward. Then he thins the upward-growing branches to reveal the inner structure of the trees. To control the tree's growth, he cuts young branch tips, called candles, in half.

Opening up the view in our garden keeps us from being cut off from people who stroll past it on the sidewalk. An unplanned but added bonus of our efforts is the encouragement we receive from these people as we work in the garden. I call these encounters "sidewalk friendships."

"To control the tree's growth, Paul cuts young branch tips, called candles, in half."

CREATING
PRIVACY

2

CREATING PRIVACY, especially in an urban or suburban area, is essential. We all need an oasis from the noise and commotion of the outside world, a special place where we can hide away and relax in solitude or with family and friends.

Fencing is the traditional solution, but how to fence the world out without feeling imprisoned within can be a dilemma. The gardens shown here demonstrate the importance of plant selection and scale when incorporating a fence into the landscape. Climbing plants and vines soften the hard edges of a fence. Trees and shrubs can actually benefit from the fence, serving as a backdrop. Plant a lush garden, add the sound of water, and you won't notice the fence or the outside world.

MICHAEL S. SCHULTZ & CHARLES W. GOODMAN

are landscape designers in Portland, Oregon. Their projects have been featured on gardening tours and in numerous magazines and books.

A Courtyard

Garden Makes a Private

Haven

A dramatic focal point helps to unify the design of a courtyard. A tiered, cast-iron fountain serves as the central element in the authors' garden.

LAWNS ARE OFTEN open, public spaces—broad, lush areas where people gather and play. Turf expanses are perhaps the most easily understood and used spaces in a garden or park. In contrast, a walled courtyard garden, which can replace lawn, affords a more singular or personal experience. Usually connected to a house or other structure, a courtyard can serve as a retreat from the larger world. Entering a walled garden tucked behind a gate, door, or screen can give a visitor a pleasant surprise.

The prospect of creating a courtyard garden was a welcome challenge for me and my partner, Will Goodman. We both were excited about exploring the process of designing and building an outdoor living room, a contained garden environment adjacent to our house.

CONSIDER EXPOSURE

Living in the Pacific Northwest, I had long dreamed of having a subtropical garden. So we wanted a courtyard with east-southwest sunlight to offer the best growing conditions for such plants.

When we were in the home-buying market, we were lucky enough to find one with the exposure we wanted. The house created an L shape, so two walls of our courtyard were already there. To complete the enclosure, we built two walls of concrete block set one upon the other, not staggered. Within this space we erected ten 9-foot-tall concrete columns linked around the top by 8-by-8-inch wood beams. We placed seven of the columns along the two concrete-block walls and spaced them far enough away from the walls to create a planting area between the columns and the walls. This double-plane effect adds depth and interest to the courtyard. The last three columns support the roof over a sitting area. This walled-in area, approximately 40 feet square, has become a space we enjoy in every season.

Any part of a yard may offer an opportunity to create a special and intimate space. Is there an area you would use more if it had privacy? Would you like to screen out a busy roadway? Can the house or garage provide some of the walls for your courtyard? Is there a door leading from the house into the area to make the space more convenient?

Consider whether the proposed courtyard will be too hot or too cold to use for a good part of the year. If your growing season is short, you may want to design your enclosed garden to enjoy maximum sun. In a warm climate, you may want to create more shade.

ENCLOSURE IS THE KEY TO A SUCCESSFUL COURTYARD

The primary element of a courtyard is the enclosed space itself, defined with walls, fencing, or plantings. The walls or borders provide structure, create a sense of depth,

Concrete block walls provide structure, privacy, and a backdrop for plantings.

An umbrella offers welcome shade.

Columns add architectural definition.

Pavers add color to the garden scheme.

Containers serve as accents and can be easily moved around a courtyard.

"Good hardscaping materials for courtyard walls include wood, stone, brick, and concrete."

Floor surfaces can be beautiful as well as functional. Large and small pavers were used in this diagonal pattern. Set in sand, individual pavers can be removed to allow for temporary plantings.

and serve as a backdrop for what will grow in the garden.

Good hardscaping materials for courtyard walls include wood, stone, brick, and concrete. When selecting materials, consider their availability, cost, and durability. Generally, a 5- to 6-foot wall provides ample height for screening and privacy. A free-standing arbor can offer additional screening in areas where only lower walls are permitted.

We constructed walls with gray, construction-grade concrete block. We wanted good structure, durability, and a "toothy" surface upon which vines could easily grow. We chose to leave the walls unpainted, but paint or stucco may be used to dress up concrete-block walls.

There are other ways to create walls for a courtyard garden. Upright wood or metal lattice screens 5 to 6 feet high and from 3 to 8 feet wide can be used to enclose a space and to support vines. As the vines grow, they'll provide privacy as well as leaves and blooms to enjoy. Hedges of boxwood or privet can also be used to create courtyard walls.

PAVING SURFACES CAN CREATE INTERESTING PATTERNS

Creating the floor of a courtyard is an interesting challenge, with many options. We decided to combine different materials to create a patterned surface. We selected three types of pavers that varied in color, texture, and size. We set the pavers in sand at a 45-degree angle in the center of the courtyard. In some areas, we used small river rock to add contrasting borders.

There are many excellent stone, brick, and concrete pavers available. Consider the color

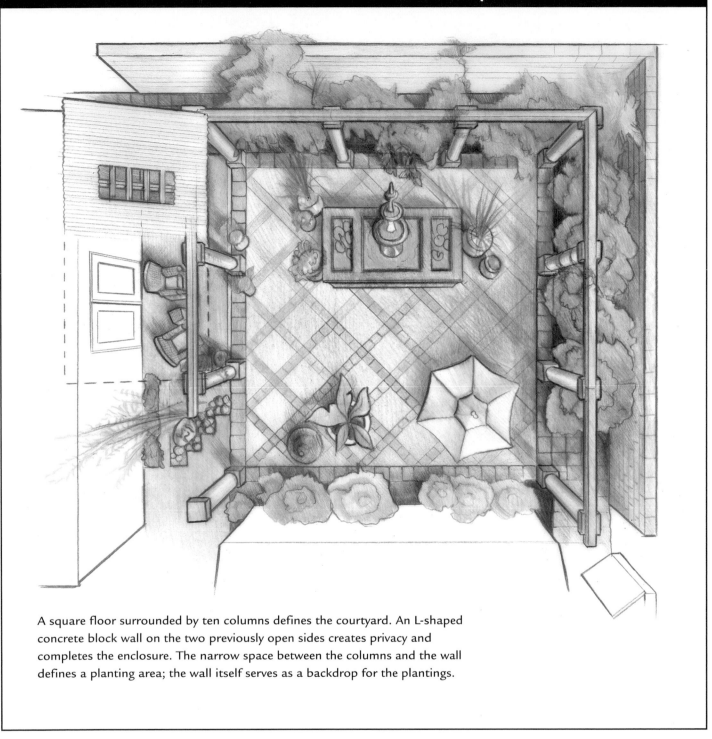

A square floor surrounded by ten columns defines the courtyard. An L-shaped concrete block wall on the two previously open sides creates privacy and completes the enclosure. The narrow space between the columns and the wall defines a planting area; the wall itself serves as a backdrop for the plantings.

Ornamental details add interest to a courtyard. A horizontal water basin makes an attractive home for goldfish and water lilies.

A small sculpture nestles amid rocks and plants.

of paving materials, both when they're dry and when they're wet. Also think of how the material will look with other colors you plan to use in your garden, as well as with the exterior colors of your house.

Pavers, stone, cobble, and brick may be set on a concrete base with mortar, or over a sub-base of gravel and then a base of construction-grade sand. We chose sand because we wanted a surface where we could plant chives, thyme, and summer annuals to grow in the

"In the winter months, when so much is dormant, the color of the wet pavers adds a touch of brightness to a gray day."

cracks, and to be able to change the layout to accommodate special plants. We may pull up a paver in spring to create a home for an annual, then replace the paver in the fall.

To set a floor in sand, soil must first be removed to allow for an ample layer of gravel as a sub-base for the sand. Setting stones or pavers in sand is much easier—and more forgiving—than working with concrete and mortar.

We were pleased with the outcome of the courtyard floor. In the winter months, when so much is dormant, the color of the wet pavers adds a touch of brightness to a gray day.

This architectural finial draws the eye with its graceful curves.

UNIFY A COURTYARD DESIGN AROUND A FOCAL POINT

Courtyards are great settings to showcase something unusual. A central element, or a focal point, is important to help establish unity in the overall design of a courtyard. A focal point gives the eye a visual resting place or destination.

A prominent location in a courtyard can be the setting for a dramatic plant or an object of special interest. A fountain or sculpture that fits the style and scale of the courtyard can serve as an excellent focal point. Fountains also add the serene sound of moving water to a garden's ambience.

Even before we found our house and started creating our courtyard, we had acquired our focal point—a tiered, 12-foot-tall, Dutch, cast-iron fountain. It served as the catalyst for the entire courtyard design. All the other elements grew from this starting point.

The fountain had to be refurbished, reassembled, and replumbed. We designed and constructed a 10-foot by 6-foot, acid-washed concrete basin as support for the fountain, and two smaller side pools for fish and tropical water lilies and lotuses. A 10-inch cap was added all around the basin to provide room for potted plants.

PLANTS ARE MORE PROTECTED NEAR COURTYARD WALLS

Planting spaces within a courtyard design are as important as the areas dedicated to hardscape. One big advantage of a courtyard garden is the favorable microclimate created by the surrounding walls. In our courtyard, the soil near the base of the walls, especially those facing north and east, tends to stay cooler and moist. Harsh winds are less likely to dry out the soil in those beds and put stress on the plants.

We created planting beds along three sides of the courtyard. Three large, deep beds along the east wall are additionally divided by rusted-steel-framed screens attached to the columns. We've planted a variety of tropical plants in these beds. In one bay, we planted angel's trumpet (*Brugmansia* 'Charles Grimaldi'), Tasmanian tree fern (*Dicksonia antarctica*), elephant ears (*Colocasia* and *Alocasia* spp.) and giant lilies (*Cardiocrinum giganteum*). In another bay, we planted various orange- and yellow-flowering *Canna* cultivars, such as 'Cleopatra' and 'Picasso', with hardy bananas (*Musa basjoo*), a windmill palm (*Trachycarpus fortunei*), and a flowering maple (*Abutilon megapotamicum*). Clematis vines (*Clematis* 'Prince Charles' and *C. spooneri*)

The use of bold columns and beams help to define planting areas. Clematis vines create a curtainlike effect for each vignette.

growing on the arbor screens create an illusion of curtains for each plant vignette.

Courtyards are also great places for potted plants. Many of the plants we wanted to use grow well in pots. We chose the pots in our courtyard for their overall size, color, design, and wear. We have enjoyed using the dwarf red Abyssinian banana (*Musa ensete*), purple glory shrub (*Tibouchina urvilleana*), and many forms of Chinese hibiscus (*Hibiscus rosa-sinensis*) in our various planters.

A walled courtyard garden affords you the creative experience of rearranging things as often as you want. We frequently move potted plants, depending on time of year and what we want to showcase.

INCLUDE SEATING AREAS

Whatever the size of your courtyard garden, it's nice to have options for seating and dining. There are numerous places to sit in our courtyard. Our favorite sitting area is a freestanding, covered structure at the north side of our courtyard. We used corrugated-metal roofing material placed over a rough-sawn wood frame and added safety glass in two areas for skylights. Cup-and-saucer vine (*Cobaea scandens*) and white passionflower (*Passiflora caerulea* 'Alba') grow up and over the structure. We use this covered area frequently for dining and as a place to just relax throughout the year.

We made sure to select several plants known for their fragrance. I especially love sitting in the courtyard on warm summer nights when the wonderfully sweet scent of angel's trumpet and giant lilies fills the air. Within this walled room, I look up to savor the faintly sparkling ceiling of sky.

Comfortable seating areas enhance the enjoyment of a walled garden. This covered structure provides sheltered seating in all types of weather.

LUCY HARDIMAN
is a garden designer,
author, and lecturer.
Her garden in Portland,
Oregon, has been
featured on television
and in many magazines
and books.

City Lot, *Pastoral* Paradise

The arbor, with its container plantings and climbing vines, offers sanctuary in a garden designed as a refuge from the city.

DURING THE 1960s, I had grand visions of creating a self-sustaining, edible landscape. I imagined a communal garden where my housemates and I would share the planting, maintenance, and harvest. In our urban oasis, we would nurture a sense of community and teach our neighbors about gardens and gardenmaking.

Today, my garden reflects just how much I've changed since then. As I became more passionate about gardening, I was no longer satisfied with vegetables alone. I still desired abundance, but now I wanted an aesthetic feast. Instead of producing food, my garden would produce peace of mind. I craved trees, shrubs, perennials, bulbs—I had to have them in profusion.

My garden (or rather, "our garden," since my tenants still share the effort) is now a far cry from its strictly edible beginnings. Encircled with an exuberant border of peren-

Brick is used throughout the garden as an element to visually
connect different gardens and provide a sense of unity.

nials, roses, and flowering shrubs, the yard provides privacy and seclusion. It is a refuge from the noise and traffic of the city, with places for relaxing, for visiting with neighbors, for hosting parties, or for sitting quietly with a good book. The garden, small as it is, has an element of mystery—a sense that more will be revealed if you linger long enough.

Of course, it took time and effort to turn a vegetable patch into a luxuriant sanctuary. To satisfy my twin desires for abundance and tranquility, I needed a garden design that would overcome two obstacles: first, the imposing scale of the buildings on and around the property, and second, the relatively small size of the backyard. I didn't want the garden to appear as if it had sprung from the land of Lilliput.

UNIFYING THE GARDEN AND BUILDINGS

My partner and I live in a 102-year-old duplex in a decidedly urban part of Portland, Oregon, and we own an adjacent fourplex on the same lot. Both buildings are huge and intimidating. Before I could consider what to plant, I had to integrate the buildings and the garden so they would work together. And since my tenants and I share the garden, I wanted everyone to have an equally enjoyable view from their windows. Creating the design was like assembling a three-dimensional puzzle—I had to think horizontally and vertically. I can't remember how many trips I made to the third-story window to get a bird's-eye view of the garden as it progressed.

My initial attempt at shaping the garden involved sweeping curves and continuous borders around the perimeter of the yard. We lived with these curves for several years, knowing all along that they didn't work with our big, square houses. Finally, I looked to the structures themselves for inspiration. The

lawn is now rectangular and very formal, echoing the shape of the buildings; we use the lawn as a croquet court, and it makes a perfect foil for the buildings and the garden.

Reshaping the lawn was the first step. Next, we looked at how hardscaping could unify the garden and anchor the houses. We had already built decks on the north side of each building, partially enclosing each one with plantings. However, the decks were separated by a narrow, muddy strip of lawn and seemed like they were in two different gardens. I wanted more visual connection between them.

This time I found inspiration in the brick walkways that meandered through the garden. We took out the sodden grass strip and built a small brick terrace to connect the decks. We also put in a brick pad as a step from one of the decks to the lawn. Across the lawn on the north side of the yard, we laid another brick pad in front of the arbor.

FITTING A LOT INTO A LITTLE GARDEN

With the framework of the garden in place, I was free to indulge my love affair with plants. To evoke a sense of richness and abundance, I

A rich mix of trees, shrubs, roses, annuals, perennials, and bulbs in a border bed creates a curtain of privacy and evokes a sense of abundance.

Luxuriant climbing vines blur the distinction between garden and buildings. Container plantings further ease the transition.

combined a variety of plants in my borders. The densely planted beds include deciduous and evergreen trees and shrubs, old roses, David Austin roses, shrub roses, perennials, annuals, and bulbs. I wanted a garden that would be interesting year-round, so I paid special attention to bark colors, textures, and berries. Many of the plants have colorful foliage in autumn and bloom into October. Shrubs with winter bloom and fragrance complete the seasonal cycle.

Because space was limited, I concentrated heavily on climbing plants and container

plantings. By making use of the space above the garden, climbing plants add lush growth without using up much ground. And since a container is, in effect, a miniature garden, containers magnify the complexity of the garden, again without taking up much room.

CLIMBING PLANTS SCREEN VIEWS

I quickly learned that the best way to reduce the perceived height of the buildings and make them an integral part of the garden landscape was to think in vertical terms. I've done this mostly through the use of vines and other climbing plants.

Luxuriant vertical growth makes it difficult to tell where the garden ends and the buildings begin. My yard is completely enclosed with green cyclone fencing—not my favorite,

"By making use of the space above the garden, climbing plants add lush growth without using up much ground."

but hardly noticeable now that it is covered in climbing roses, clematis, and vines. Likewise, nobody ever sees the downspouts on my house in summer, because they are well camouflaged by flowering annual vines.

The arbor at the edge of the lawn is home to *Rosa* 'New Dawn' and *Clematis* 'Elsa Spath'. Last year, in an attempt to create more enclosure and privacy, we built a structure that abuts the long fence line on the north. Climbers tangle and weave their way along the fence and up this structure, which repeats the architectural style of the arbor. *Rosa glauca* is paired with *Clematis recta* 'Purpurea', and C. 'Royalty' scrambles along the fence. At the far end of the fence, nightshade vine (*Solanum crispum* 'Glasnevin') consorts with 'Mrs. Oakley Fisher' rose.

The arbor serves as an intermediary, something in between the scale of the ground plantings and that of the surrounding buildings. Small trees and large shrubs further break up the vertical scale and also make companionable hosts for vines.

In the back border, *Clematis orientalis* threads its way through beautyberry (*Callicarpa bodinieri* 'Profusion'). Nearby, a lovely *Styrax japonica* is home to *Clematis macropetala* 'Maidwell Hall'; at the other end of the garden, C. × 'Campanulina Plena' clambers up through the branches of a Carolina silverbells (*Halesia carolina*). Growing over the top of our garage, supported by grapevines, is C. 'Venosa Violacea', and several varieties of honeysuckle (*Lonicera*) and an espaliered quince scale the walls of our building.

Whenever I enter the garden, I am immediately made aware that the plants growing vertically are the ones that frame and enclose the garden, creating a wondrous feeling of sanctuary.

'New Dawn' climbing rose and 'Elsa Spath' clematis animate the arbor and add fine detail to the wooden structure.

CONTAINER PLANTINGS OFFER A MOVABLE FEAST

My collection of more than 60 terra-cotta planters serves a variety of purposes. One group of containers greets and invites you to climb the front steps; another planter beckons you to wander down a path. I've grouped some pots as focal points at the foot of the arbor, and others frame a brick seating area under a large apple tree filled with clematis vines. A single terra-cotta pot on a simple circle of brick forms the intersection of several converging paths. In a corner of a deck, large pots provide screening and privacy from the building next door.

Containers are everywhere in my garden, lush and verdant, filled with annuals, perennials, grasses, roses, topiaried ivy, vines, and shrubs. Asiatic and Oriental lilies are fragrant and surprising additions to planters. Cannas, acidantheras, and tuberoses thrive in pots and create wonderful focal points. I also use lots of variegated foliage in containers, especially in those that will be placed in shady spots.

When in doubt, I always overplant; skimpy and sparse simply won't do in this garden.

Here, containers are not just ornaments, but an integral part of a garden design that is still evolving. I rely on them not the least because they can be picked up and moved around. They're the perfect partners in my quest for greater abundance and a more idyllic urban paradise.

Planting in layers creates visual interest and dimension.

Accents, such as a tutelage, serve as focal points.

Container plantings allow for more plants where space is limited.

A brick pad provides a transition between the deck and lawn.

ALICE S. WAEGEL

A biology professor at Neumann College, Alice Waegel belongs to several gardening societies and lectures and writes about gardening from her home in Pennsylvania.

Hang, Stack, Trellis

Stacks of small clay pots create a tripod to lift trailing annuals. Variegated common periwinkle, lobelia, and English ivy cascade from pots while impatiens, nicotiana, violas, and tuberous begonias provide color.

WHEN I VISITED the gardens of southern England, I was mesmerized by the weathered walls dripping with flowering plants. Plants spilled over the tops of walls everywhere, even at the bed-and-breakfasts. And there was more to catch the eye: ancient sculptured hedges, exquisite topiaries, and elevated urns. These vertical statements in the English gardens increased visual interest and often added a measure of privacy.

I have tried to adapt the English use of vertical gardening surfaces in my own small, suburban lot in southeastern Pennsylvania. One of my alternatives to walls and hedges has been multilevel container gardening. This solution may be less permanent than a stone wall, but it can be affordable and imaginative.

A simple log can make a handsome pedestal. A pot of tuberous begonias is brought to eye level by being placed on a log, and impatiens spill from flues cut to different lengths.

PUTTING PLANTS ON A PEDESTAL

Climbing vines, hanging baskets, and raised containers on inexpensive pedestals, such as inverted pots and tree logs, supply me with a good deal of vertical drama at a moderate cost.

Logs

Initially, I elevated some of my patio containers on tree logs, 8 to 12 inches in diameter. I set these logs on end to raise my containers several feet. Just one word of caution: Always inspect a log for insects before including it in the garden.

Since my patio is shady, I created a trailing effect partly with perennial vines, such as English ivy (*Hedera helix*) and blue-flowering common periwinkle (*Vinca minor*), which stay green throughout the seasons and provide winter interest. I also added the cascading, deep blue and white-flowered edging lobelia (*Lobelia erinus* 'Sapphire Pendula' and *L. erinus* 'White Cascade'). In sunnier spots, I edged containers with annual sweet alyssum; the tiny, pinkish white daisies of *Erigeron karvinskianus*; and perennial aubrieta with its simple, spring-blooming lavender and purple flowers.

Inverted pots

Besides logs, I also create pedestals from inverted terra-cotta pots or less expensive polypropylene nursery pots. Although polypropylene is not particularly attractive, the black color is unobtrusive, and you can disguise it with vigorous vines such as blue-flowering greater periwinkle (*Vinca major* 'Variegata'), with its green leaves with creamy white margins.

I achieve an elegant effect with terra-cotta by inverting a single large pot as a pedestal and topping it off with a matching upright pot. In my garden, I have three such arrangements filled with ferns, hostas, vincas, and variegated euonymus.

Another approach is a tripod support made from three stacks of inverted, smaller pots. In a third approach, I created a tiered plant wall with inverted pots, elevating several rectangular planters to different heights.

TALL PLANTS ADD DRAMA

Another inexpensive way I add height to my container garden is to grow trees and shrubs in large pots. A tightfisted gardener can buy these plants inexpensively at yearly nursery sales. Although a bit risky here in USDA Hardiness Zone 6 (−10°F), nursery stock I purchased at a 75 percent discount in November has flourished with a little coddling and winter protection. I have been particularly happy with conical dwarf Alberta spruce (*Picea glauca* 'Sander's Blue'), which provides screening and interest year-round.

Other favorites include purple-leaf sand cherry (*Prunus* × *cistena*), which has fragrant, pale pink spring flowers and purple foliage, and Japanese maple (*Acer palmatum* 'Atropurpureum') for its bright red fall color.

Trees, such as *Acer palmatum* cvs., can be grown in containers for dramatic effect.

Trellises provide a backdrop and sense of enclosure. Sweet peas and black-eyed-Susan vines lace up supports behind the seating area in the author's garden. A pot of impatiens is ornamented with a pair of whimsical clay frogs.

"By using a combination of methods to create a multilevel container garden on my patio, I have produced a lush and beautiful setting without depleting my gardening budget."

For shade containers, I prefer deciduous shrubs like variegated, big-leaf hydrangea (*Hydrangea macrophylla* 'Mariessii Variegata'), with its large, mauve flower heads, and summer-sweet (*Clethra alnifolia*), which has a lovely late-summer scent and white, brushlike flowers.

VINES AND PLANT WALLS

Along with trees and shrubs, I make space for perennial and annual vines, which can be trained upward to eye level and above. I fashion an inexpensive tripod out of bamboo canes for vines such as the fragrant annual sweet peas (*Lathyrus odoratus*). Another annual vine easy to grow on bamboo canes is the black-eyed-Susan vine (*Thunbergia alata*)—I like the cultivar that bears pale yellow flowers with dark centers.

You can also support vines on pea sticks, which cost nothing at all if you have a supply of bushy twigs, and trellises that you can make by yourself or purchase from a local garden center. In one of my containers, I use a simple, homemade trellis to support the yellow and pink flowers and medium green, pointed oval leaves of 'Goldflame' honeysuckle (*Lonicera heckrottii* 'Goldflame').

You can grow an entire wall of vines by placing wood lattice in long, rectangular containers before planting. When the vines grow up the lattice, they form a privacy screen and vertical interest. I have created a similar effect, perhaps even more lush, with a plant wall—basically a wooden frame covered with chicken wire or lattice and filled with peat or compost. My wall is a colorful abundance of impatiens, lobelia and browallia that blocks an undesirable view.

HANGING BASKETS

Hanging baskets provide the finishing touch in my garden. I like to hang plants in places other than from a typical overhang or wall hook; I use tree branches, poles, and posts instead. I support three more hanging baskets with two metal hanger stands and the metal post of a birdhouse. Hanger stands, which are poles with a shepherd's crook on the top and a supporting foot on the bottom, can be inserted into any available square foot of ground and are reasonably priced. I placed mine next to the plant wall and hung the plants at different levels to provide maximum aesthetic appeal. To avoid an overly fussy effect, I repeat many of the same annuals in my hanging containers that I use in other patio plantings.

By using a combination of methods to create a multilevel container garden on my patio, I have produced a lush and beautiful setting without depleting my gardening budget. My yard now has a sense of enclosure and privacy provided by my vertical containers. But the most important benefit of the added dimensions is the increased drama, which in a small way brings me back to the gardens of southern England.

Plants Enclose
an In-Town Lot

DAVID ELLIS

owns Ellis LanDesign, a landscape architecture firm in Atlanta.

A limbed-up holly anchors one corner of the front yard, screening power lines yet not making the lawn and garden feel too closed in. (#1 on site plan.)

MANY URBAN residential environments, despite their advantages, are cursed with an excess of asphalt, noise, and unsightly views. So for those of us who live in cities, there is much to be said for creating a private oasis, no matter how small the plot. Fortunately, I live on a street where the small yards are given mostly to lawn. Mine happened to be a weedy lawn, accented by little more than a few foundation shrubs, so the possibilities were endless for creating my own garden from scratch.

Out front, I wanted to block the views of the cars, driveways, and power poles that line both sides of the street, and I wanted to create a sense of semiprivacy in the garden, while keeping the front door visible and accessible to visitors. Out back, I saw an opportunity for total privacy. To pull this off, I used a variety of enclosures—mostly green ones, accented or supported by a few structures—to mark the boundaries of my yard. By doing this, I've created a garden that is private on the inside and intriguing from the outside.

TALL PLANTINGS HIDE POWER LINES

To enclose the front garden, I started by planting large shrubs and trees at the property corners to screen the power lines from view. I did this with evergreen Burford and Foster's hollies (*Ilex cornuta* 'Burfordii', and *I. × attenuata* 'Foster #2) and the deciduous *Hydrangea paniculata* 'Tardiva'. I limbed up their multiple trunks to screen the power lines without completely blocking the view of the sidewalk. Also, the sculptural trunks are eye-catching.

Developing a Strategy

The author did not want to make his urban Atlanta home a walled-in fortress. Instead, he opted for a mixture of plants and fences to screen but not totally shut out surrounding views.

Photos taken from numbered positions.

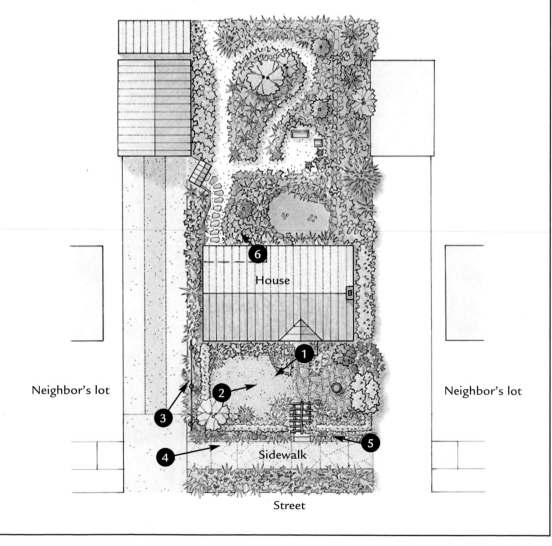

Neighbor's lot

Neighbor's lot

House

Sidewalk

Street

From the street, these limbed-up trees and shrubs add a greater sense of depth as you look through them toward the house, making my tiny front yard seem just a little bigger. They also offer a backdrop for other plantings—annuals, perennials, and evergreen groundcovers. Over time, as these anchor plants mature and create a shadier environment, I am replacing the sun-loving perennials and annuals with shade-loving perennials and ground covers.

Along one side in the front, I expanded this concept of mixed, layered plantings by establishing a screen of evergreen and deciduous plants from the corner of the lot to the house. Evergreen hollies and a chaste tree

(*Vitex agnus-castus*) step down to *Hydrangea macrophylla* 'Ayesha' and other flowering shrubs, annuals, and perennials to create a pocket garden anchored by a small birdbath.

A LOW HEDGE PROVIDES SEMI-PRIVACY

Along the front edge of my shrinking lawn, I planted a low hedge of European beeches (*Fagus sylvatica*), though American beeches (*F. grandifolia*) would have been an equally good selection if they had been available at local nurseries at planting time. Both of these beeches can grow quite tall, but they are also easily maintained as a hedge if planted closely,

You can barely see the neighbor's front yard through this screening, which includes deciduous and evergreen trees, a low hedge, and annuals and perennials. (#2 on site plan.)

Flowers in spring, screening in summer, views in winter. When the climbing roses, clematis vines, and neighboring trees drop their foliage in late fall, the author can see the Atlanta skyline from his house. To create a framework for the flowering vines and canes, decorative yet functional steel rods (INSET) are driven through long-lasting locust posts. (#3 on site plan.)

pruned selectively in winter, and sheared a couple of times during the growing season.

I chose the beeches for several reasons. In addition to fitting the style of my cottage garden, they could be easily kept under 4 feet in height, which was important in the front yard, where I wanted something low enough to permit views both in and out of the garden.

Also, I wanted something different from the traditional boxwood, holly, or privet hedge. Though beeches are commonly grown in the South, you don't often see them maintained as hedges. These beeches hold on to their leaves until early spring, when they put out delicate new growth that shimmers in the sunlight. In summer, the leaves are a rich green, and in the fall, they turn a beautiful golden color.

The fence is constructed from three large black locust (*Robinia pseudoacacia*) posts with several steel rods driven through them horizontally. The black locust has a straight trunk and is slow to rot, making it ideal for fence posts and rails. Though it's most commonly sold as split rails, I was able to obtain some unsplit logs.

The fence is draped with 'Mermaid' and 'New Dawn' roses and accented with several clematis vines, which make a fine spring show and provide plenty of dense, green foliage for screening throughout the summer. At their feet, on the public side, is a bed filled with colorful annuals and perennials.

PLANT BOTH SIDES OF A FENCE

For instant enclosure around a garden space, fencing is a clear alternative to hedges. In the backyard, where I could have used tall, solid plank fencing for privacy, I opted instead for hog-wire fencing strung between locust posts, to keep the dogs in check. Hog-wire fencing is exactly what you'd expect—rolls of wire fencing (with larger squares than those of hardware cloth or chicken wire) used by farmers to keep in hogs. And though I don't think it makes a bad-looking fence, I planted both sides to create a lush, living wall that I find more interesting than almost any kind of fence because of the varied textures and the way it changes throughout the seasons.

That said, I recently added a small section of bamboo fencing along the back property line that I like specifically for its texture and the way it adds to the Asian theme I've been developing in my rear garden. I stumbled across this bamboo in an import shop, where it had been used as packing material.

Plantings can beautify a fence as well as soften its hard lines. In tight situations, all you need is a few inches of planting area to

A VINE-DRAPED FENCE OFFERS SEASONAL VIEWS

In winter, when the leaves have fallen from the neighborhood trees, I have a wonderful view of the Atlanta skyline. To preserve this view, I enclosed the south side of the front yard with open fencing draped in vines that drop their leaves once cold weather arrives.

"Though there's limited space between the backyard fence and a driveway shared with neighbors, I've worked in a mix of narrow, upright shrubs, perennials, and shade-tolerant vines."

grow vines that can be trained along a fence. Though there's limited space between the backyard fence and a driveway shared with neighbors, I've worked in a mix of narrow, upright shrubs, perennials, and shade-tolerant vines like five-leaf akebia (*Akebia quinata*). Inside the fence, where there's a bit more room, I'm growing more Foster's hollies along with a variety of other favorite plants.

The rear gate, which leads from the driveway to the backyard garden, is Asian inspired. The doors were rescued from a junk pile, and the rest of the structure, including the tin roof, was built to accommodate them. Unlike the open gate and arbor out front, this solid gate sends the message that this is my private retreat in the heart of the city.

Mixed plantings screen a hog-wire fence that keeps the dogs in the yard. The gate, bamboo edging, and plantings show a clear Asian influence. (#6 on site plan.)

Turn Your Sidewalk into a Garden Room

If you're fortunate enough to have a sidewalk, you have the perfect spot for a garden area you can share with your neighbors. By planting both sides of my sidewalk with a mix of small trees, flowering shrubs, and perennials, I created a garden that rarely fails to slow down passersby. Since this is considered public space, it pays to keep a few things in mind when you plant this area.

Neighbors can enjoy the changing seasons in this pass-through garden bordering both sides of the front walk. (#4 on site plan.)

- Choose trees that can mature comfortably in tight spaces. Persian ironwood (*Parrotia persica*), Kousa dogwood (*Cornus kousa*), and yaupon holly (*Ilex vomitoria*) have worked well for me.

- Keep in mind that as the trees mature, your once-sunny area will become shadier and you will probably have to change some of the underplantings.

- Include lots of bulbs for early spring color. Squill (*Scilla* spp. and cvs.), daffodils (*Narcissus* spp. and cvs.), and snowdrops (*Galanthus* spp. and cvs.) are all good choices.

- Include flowering shrubs—both evergreen and deciduous—that either take well to pruning or won't get too wide. Be keen on pruning, keeping in mind that scraggly branches can be an annoyance to those trying to park their cars.

- Add some self-sowing annuals such as spider flower (*Cleome hassleriana*), cockscomb (*Celosia* spp. and cvs.), or love-lies-bleeding (*Amaranthus caudatus*) for a splash of color throughout the summer.

- Keep in mind that the sidewalk strip tends to dry out more quickly than the rest of the garden. Be prepared to water, plant drought-tolerant species, or consider berming this area to create a slightly raised bed.

- Design several crossover areas so that people parking in front of your house can step out onto paving or stone instead of onto plants.

Rich plantings signal an in-town oasis. Though the plantings are designed primarily to create a semiprivate front-yard garden, they look just as good from the street as from the house. (#5 on site plan.)

From Tiny Yard to Private Paradise

VERLE LESSIG

Verle Lessig (1947-2000), was co-owner of The Fertile Delta, a garden center in Chicago, IL. His passion for gardening and unusual plants was reflected in the stock offered at the center and by his own garden.

Viewing the garden from a second story deck gave the author a vantage point from which he could monitor the garden's progress and make necessary changes.

I TRAVEL FROM CALIFORNIA to Florida and from Oregon to Long Island looking for exotic plants. As the part owner of a garden center, it's one of the most enjoyable parts of my job— discovering all those fantastic tropicals, exotic evergreens, and interesting trees. But for years it was also frustrating. I lived in an apartment, and having a garden was out of the question.

So, about six years ago, I bought a house with a small yard in a neighborhood of Chicago. My tiny patch of turf looked like all of the other postage-stamp-sized yards on the block, but I saw something else: a private retreat filled with my favorite plants, a place that would feel far from city skyscrapers, where the gentle splash of water drowned out the urban din. All I had to do was turn this vision into reality. The backyard was only 25 by 50 feet, but I was going to make the most of it.

A SUNKEN PATIO
FEELS SECLUDED

The first thing that I wanted to do was to make the yard feel secluded. Local regulations permitted fences to be no higher than 6 feet; I knew that this wouldn't be enough, but I installed one anyway. Then, I dug out an area a foot deep for a patio about 10 feet wide and 20 feet long. With the patio sunken below ground level, the fence would seem higher, so the patio would feel more secluded. It also meant that it would be necessary to install a drainage system to direct excess rainwater into a nearby catch basin. Next to the patio I wanted a pond, so I dug an adjoining 6-by-12-foot area another 2½ feet deep.

The excavated soil was trundled over by wheelbarrow to help fill in the berms that I was building around the outer edge of the yard. I laid two courses of cinder blocks along the bottom of the fence, then piled the soil so that it gradually sloped down about 2 feet toward the pond and the patio to create a perfect planting bed. In effect, the berms turned the yard into an amphitheater.

While building the berms, I hauled in a few artificial boulders to edge a newly built stream, to create a waterfall, and to serve as outcrops. It took a lot of tinkering to make it all look natural. I sometimes checked the progress by running upstairs to a second-story deck to get a good overview.

Those bird's-eye views also helped when I was laying the patio. I handpicked the flagstones to get colors and textures to match the artificial rocks, and I wanted them laid out in just the right mix of shapes and sizes. I knew good hardscaping was crucial to the success of my project, and that high vantage point helped me to see how everything tied together.

USE TREES AND SHRUBS
AS A SCREEN

Once the berms were built, the patio was laid, and the pond was lined, I started planting the outer edges of my urban oasis with trees and shrubs. The woody plants would hide my view of the fence and tower over it, adding to the garden's feeling of seclusion. To make an effective screen, I positioned groups of trees more closely together than nursery people usually advise. To avoid being rapidly overrun, I selected mostly dwarf or slow-growing trees. But I didn't worry too much about the ultimate size of everything I planted—that would have made the choices in my small yard too limited. A few of the trees will eventually grow out of bounds; when they do, I'll prune them back or dig them out. I plan to let a few trees grow over a pathway to heighten the sense of privacy. I selected trees with at least two seasons of interest. Most were chosen for their foliage; I like anything variegated or with unusual colors or leaves.

I planted 17 trees in the yard, and underplanted them with about 20 shrubs. Then, to thicken my privacy screen even more, I planted about 15 different clematis, which scramble freely over the fence and some trees and shrubs.

DECORATE WITH FLOWERS

To make my privacy screen more decorative, I try to choose plants with interesting foliage and flowers. With bulbs, perennials, and

"A few of the trees will eventually grow out of bounds; when they do, I'll prune them back or dig them out."

(ABOVE) Trees leaning over the paths give the garden a sense of secrecy. Large trees add a special touch to a small garden.

(RIGHT) To create a rich, lush look, the author planted trees, shrubs, perennials, and bulbs closely together.

Trees add privacy.

Colorful foliage
provides long-lasting
interest.

Evergreens add
visual interest
year-round.

Plants grown
between flagstones
create a naturalized
effect.

A small pond
expands plant
possibilities.

> *"I've never been sentimental about tearing out anything that doesn't perform well or look good."*

annuals, I prefer blues and purples to brassy golds and yellows, but that's my personal taste. I filled the open spaces along the berms with perennials and old-fashioned annuals like love-in-a-mist (*Nigella damascena*) and larkspur (*Delphinium* spp.) that self-sow. I like all sorts of tropicals too, so I use them in containers to dress up the area and add interest to the patio.

I was careful to avoid plants that would quickly outgrow the scale of my garden. I like hardy hibiscus (*Hibiscus moscheutos*), for example, but, in my tiny garden, something with a flower the size of a dinner plate just doesn't look right. Also, because my space is limited, I've never been sentimental about tearing out anything that doesn't perform well or look good.

My garden is still evolving. Every time something at the garden center strikes my fancy I bring it home and put it in the ground. Last spring, I made an inspiring visit to Holland at the height of the tulip season, and this spring my garden will be full of tulips. I'm not saying it's going to look like a Dutch masterpiece, but I can say this—it doesn't look like it's in Chicago either.

Water Features Add Tranquility

The water garden played a key role in my design. It adds to the tranquil, countrified feeling I wanted to create. And the waterfall at the head of the stream provides a nice sound that drowns out the noise that is part of any city neighborhood. The pond and stream banks also give me the chance to grow water plants.

COMPELLING
GARDEN SPACES

3

THERE ARE AS MANY WAYS TO DESIGN A GARDEN as there are gardeners. Presented here are some outstanding examples of gardens that demonstrate the principles for creating a small garden—not just private retreats but also front-yard gardens where the space is more public. Here, there are opportunities to create places that invite the neighbors to linger and chat over the proverbial fence.

While these gardens may vary in their styles, maintenance demands, plant choices, and moods, all of them reflect the lifestyles of their owners, and all of them encourage visitors to linger and enjoy them with all of their senses—sight, hearing, smell, touch, and, in some cases, even taste. We hope that you find inspiration for creating your own garden—no matter how small the lot.

JENI WEBBER

has been gardening for 20 years and is a residential landscape architect and horticulturalist in Oakland, California.

Front-Yard
Gardens Make a Strong
First Impression

The effect of front-yard gardens extends beyond their boundaries, enhancing the whole neighborhood.

FRONT-YARD GARDENS can change neighborhoods. I've witnessed this both as a gardener and as a landscape architect. Years ago, I mixed some annuals and perennials among the evergreen foundation shrubs in front of my family's home. Before long, the welcoming curves I had carved out of the sod near our front door extended through a series of planting beds and paths to our neighbors' yards on either side. We shared plants, time, and friendship with those neighbors. And passersby encouraged my gardening efforts. I felt that I was doing more than just sprucing up our front yard. I was making our neighborhood a friendlier place to live.

DIFFERENT STYLES, ONE NEIGHBORHOOD

Now that I'm a professional garden designer, I keep this mission in mind. There is an older neighborhood in Palo Alto, California, where I've designed four front-yard gardens.

∼ Cottage Style ∼

A picket fence and a profusion of plants create a cozy setting

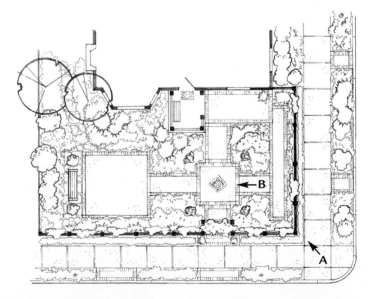

A picket fence was set back from the sidewalk so that flower beds could be planted on either side. (A on site plan.)

True to cottage-garden style, the front yard is laid out on cross axes. At one end, there's a bench where people can sit and enjoy the garden. (B on site plan.)

Bob McIntyre's charming house on a small corner lot was the perfect setting for a cottage garden. It was also in keeping with his longing for a small lawn bordered by flowers and a picket fence. Focal points include a bench from which he can enjoy the garden and the Sunday paper, lemon trees in large pots, and a birdbath, which is placed at the intersection of two paths. A rose-covered arbor over the front gate greets guests upon their arrival, and an herb garden borders the walk to the front door.

Like any good cottage garden, this one boasts a profusion of plants. We chose a bright, cheerful color scheme—yellow, orange, and red. Black-eyed Susans (*Rudbeckia fulgida* var. *sullivantii* 'Goldstrum') anchor the garden in summer; nasturtiums (*Tropaeolum majus* cvs.) and *Lobelia* cvs. grow in an untamed riot against the fence. Large clumps of ornamental grasses and rows of lavender (*Lavandula angustifolia* 'Hidcote') help soften the strong color scheme.

So that the garden can be enjoyed both from the street and from the yard, we planted both sides of the fence, as well as the grassy strip between the sidewalk and street. This gives neighbors out for their morning walk a sense of moving through a garden, instead of just looking over the fence at one.

Although they are very different, they all suit the neighborhood just fine. One is a cottage-style home on a street corner, where I added a picket fence, arbor, herb garden, birdbath, and lots of colorful plantings. There's even a bench for sitting in the garden, and the fence is low enough that conversations can take place over it. Just down the street is a Craftsman bungalow, and I've treated the hardscaping with similar craftsmanship, while keeping the plantings simple yet attractive.

Across the street is a one-story ranch with contemporary landscaping—lots of curving beds, ornamental grasses, and low-maintenance perennials. And finally, just a few blocks away, is a traditional Colonial with a formal landscape featuring a brick walk, symmetric foundation plantings, and a picket fence draped in roses. All four front-yard gardens have small patches of lawn, but the foundation plantings are varied, and the gardens are designed to suit the houses as well as the gardening abilities of the homeowners.

Any front garden could benefit from this kind of attention. What would be most appropriate for your house? Maybe you have a cedar split-rail fence that would look nice knee-deep in daylilies and laced with rambling roses. Or a stuccoed courtyard wall with alcoves that would benefit from a water feature or an attractive arrangement of desert plants. Or even an old Victorian in a western ski town that could be enhanced with native wildflowers.

LEAD GUESTS TO THE DOOR

Of course, before you get carried away with planting, you have to take care of a couple of practical matters. And the first of those is to clearly identify the front door, so that when guests arrive, they know exactly where to go.

"Whether you're working with existing plantings or starting from scratch, go for variety, even among evergreens."

When I visited Dublin, Ireland, I marveled at how homeowners distinguished their row houses by painting the front door a favorite color. You can do this, too. In addition, there are a number of other ways you can give your place personality: by building an arbor over your entrance, by grouping several eye-catching containers on either side of your door, by installing a sculpture or wall fountain in an entry courtyard, or by growing a vine up and over your doorway. You can even install special landscape lighting (beyond the standard porch lights and lampposts) to highlight your entry at night.

To reach the doorway, you need a good path. Build one that's wide enough for two people to walk abreast. It should also be safe—that is, with an even, nonslip surface that won't cause anyone to stumble or fall.

Poured concrete is the most commonly used path material because of its low cost. However, other materials like brick, stone, and concrete pavers make a stronger first impression and are often more appropriate in a garden setting. Even concrete that has been stained or texturized is much more interesting than plain concrete, and is still very affordable. Or spruce up existing concrete paths by edging them with bricks or cobblestones. Select materials that match the style, materials, or colors of your house. This will better integrate your house and landscape.

Colonial Style

Traditional plants and structured paths tie a symmetrically designed house to its garden

A mother of four children, Selena Dwight wanted to create a sense of order in front of her Colonial home that wasn't always possible indoors. She had already redesigned the bedlines in front of this traditionally styled home. My job was to design the plantings. I also added the picket fence and arbor, and edged the neatly manicured lawn with bricks to match the front walk, which really helped tie the house and landscape together. These hardscaping elements also gave structure to the garden.

In keeping with the historic style of the house, we focused on plants that were traditional in Colonial times. Boxwoods were the most obvious choice for establishing a foundation of evergreens. Roses were planted against the fence, which features hoop arches to give them additional support as they grow. *Clematis montana* combines nicely with the roses, which will grow up to cover the arbor. Lavender, punctuated with standard roses for a touch of formality, anchor the beds on either side of the front porch. All of the plantings are carefully balanced to suit the symmetry of the house. And finally, we added a small cutting garden in the sunny side yard, which is accessed from the front yard.

A formal, symmetrical garden suits this Colonial house. The plantings in the beds that flank the entryway mirror each other. (A on site plan.)

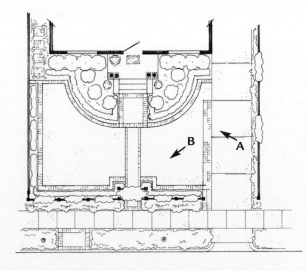

(LEFT) An elegantly designed arbor signals the entrance to this front-yard garden. Soon it will be draped in clematis and roses. (B on site plan.)

Bungalow Style

Hardscaping reflects the Arts and Crafts aesthetic

Dave Ketchum is an avid gardener. So although I designed his front-yard garden, he handled the installation and does all the gardening. Our goal was to design a garden that complemented the architecture of the renovated bungalow. In particular, we wanted the hardscaping to reflect a sense of quality craftsmanship. We added brick bands to widen the existing driveway and paths. And for variety, we laid tumbled bluestone for lawn edging, which is wide enough to serve as a path in wet weather.

My planting design goals were fourfold: to complement the green walls, to create structure with plants, to diversify the plantings so that there are stars in each season, and to minimize maintenance. A mixed border of evergreen and deciduous shrubs, small trees, perennials, and ornamental grasses surrounds the small lawn.

Many of the deciduous shrubs display colorful bark and interesting branching structure in winter. And lime-green and wine-colored foliage are used to complement the green stucco walls. The dark foliage of Japanese barberry

Brick bands both widen and dress up the driveway and front paths. Plantings are designed to complement the color of the walls. (A on site plan.)

(INSET) Tumbled bluestone lawn edging does double duty; in rainy weather, it also serves as a path. (B on site plan.)

(*Berberis thunbergii f. atropurpurea*), spurge (*Euphorbia dulcis* 'Chameleon'), and coral bells (*Heuchera micrantha* var. *diversifolia* 'Palace Purple') contrast wonderfully with the bright yellow leaves of Bowles' golden sedge (*Carex elata* 'Aurea') and golden creeping Jenny (*Lysimachia nummularia* 'Aurea').

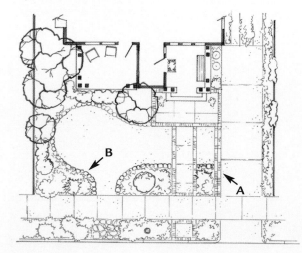

Most front-yard paths are straight because they are the easiest for contractors to build and the quickest route to the front door. Curved or jogged paths are often more interesting, especially when they wind their way through a garden, toward a birdbath, or alongside a bench. Most front paths lead either to the street or to the driveway, usually to the place where most people park. In many cases, however, two paths make more sense, even if one is little more than a stepping-stone path that runs alongside the driveway to the street.

ENHANCE FOUNDATION PLANTINGS FOR YEAR-ROUND GOOD LOOKS

Once you've highlighted your entry and established your pathways, you can concentrate on the plantings. The most significant are those planted at the foundation, where the house meets the ground. This is a wonderful place to create multiseason interest and plant your first front-yard garden.

Start by evaluating what you have. If your living room hasn't seen the light of day for 20 years, you might want to start by ripping out overgrown shrubs. But most of the time, you can work with what you have. Mature camellias (*Camellia* spp.) and hollies (*Ilex* spp.), for instance, might be limbed up into small trees—especially if they anchor corners of the house or either side of the front door—while ungainly rhododendrons (*Rhododendron* spp.) or boxwoods (*Buxus sempervirens*) could be drastically pruned and allowed to regrow beneath windows. Healthy shrubs that no longer suit the site might be transplanted to other places in the yard.

"To reach the doorway, you need a good path. Build one that's wide enough for two people to walk abreast."

Whether you're working with existing plantings or starting from scratch, go for variety, even among evergreens. Select shrubs and small trees with different leaf shapes, textures, foliage color, and growth habits.

Also, think in terms of "mixed border" instead of strictly "evergreen foundation plantings." Starting with a base of well-spaced evergreen groupings, highlight spring with bulbs, flowering shrubs, and small flowering trees; summer with splashes of perennials and annuals; autumn with bright foliage; and winter with berries, seed heads, and interesting bark. Consider the flaming leaves of burning bush (*Euonymus alatus*), the red stems and yellow leaves of redtwig dogwood (*Cornus alba* 'Aurea'), or the scarlet berries of winterberry (*Ilex verticillata*), then add bold masses or bright splashes of your favorite flowers.

PLANT ONLY WHAT YOU CAN MANAGE

When creating a front-yard garden, it's important to consider how much upkeep will be required. It's all right to allow a back-yard garden to grow wild and woolly at times, but since the front garden is always on display, you want to keep it looking as good as possible. Although ideally you might envision a lush mixed border embracing all sides of the garden—and this could be your goal—it may be best to start with a small area and see just how much effort it takes to maintain.

In addition to planting only as much as you know you can tend, avoid high-maintenance plants that need frequent watering, are susceptible to pests and diseases, or require daily deadheading. Instead, choose from among easy-care plants with a long season of interest. Black-eyed Susans (*Rudbeckia* spp.), daylilies (*Hemerocallis* cvs.), coneflowers (*Echinacea* spp.), and ornamental grasses like sedges (*Carex* spp.), fountain grasses (*Pennisetum*

~ Contemporary Style ~

Curved beds complement a contemporary ranch house

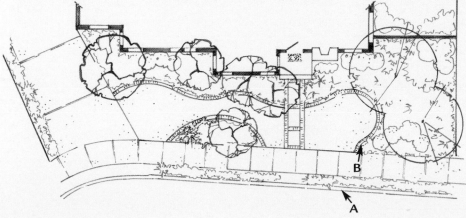

(ABOVE) Ornamental grasses, flowering shrubs, and daylilies anchor low-maintenance plantings in front of this contemporary ranch. (A on site plan.)

(RIGHT) Beds were edged in brick to look neat and to complement the front walk. (B on site plan.)

spp.), and *Miscanthus sinensis* are excellent choices for much of the country.

Another trick is to give your plantings a backdrop or a structure upon which to grow. Plant a long border beside a fence or in front of a retaining wall. Incorporate a mailbox in a curved bed that links the driveway and street. Allow perennial beds to creep into or border your front path. Plant some flowering vines—perhaps a climbing rose and a clematis—to scramble up your lamppost. Although not all plantings need a backdrop—freestanding island beds are a good example—such solid elements help carry the garden through the winter when herbaceous plants are dormant.

Structures should complement, not compete with, the architecture of your house. Use similar materials, like a brick mailbox post and paths if you have a Colonial home, a white picket fence if you live in a cozy cottage, or a stacked-stone wall if you hang your hat in a New England saltbox.

So if you've been dreaming of a front-yard garden, go ahead. There's absolutely nothing that says you have to stick strictly with the ubiquitous American lawn and evergreen foundation shrubs, a greatly overrated trend started in the late 1800s. Even if you keep the lawn and shrubs, which certainly have their merits, you can still spruce things up by expanding your foundation plantings, adding a few flower beds, draping your mailbox in vines, or placing a couple of colorful pots on the porch. And finally, take time to enjoy your front-yard garden. Welcome the opportunity it brings for meeting new neighbors. After all, there may be some fellow gardeners among them.

In the process of renovating their house, Patty and Jim White decided to update their garden as well. They wanted to revamp all the plantings, retaining only two large loquats (*Eriobotrya japonica*), a row of tall cedars, and an old rose climbing the chimney.

To complement the contemporary house, we opted for a series of curved beds with sweeping paths of lawn between them.

Low-maintenance was a top priority. They welcomed the use of less traditional plants, like ornamental grasses and New Zealand flax (*Phormium tenax*). An olive tree anchored the planting scheme, and we added a mix of plants with gray-green and wine-colored foliage. We planted the sidewalk strip with low-maintenance plants such as lavender, irises, and ornamental grasses.

"Avoid high-maintenance plants that need frequent watering, are susceptible to diseases, or require daily deadheading."

CHRIS D. MOORE

is a landscape architect
with Jack Chandler and
Associates, a practice in
the Napa, California,
region.

A
Front-Yard
Retreat

In a small front yard,
concrete pads outlined
with brick lead to the
courtyard designed and
built by the author.
The stone wall shelters
a patio and fountain
without looking like a
blank fortress.

O N A SMALL PROPERTY, the front
yard is precious. Usually it's gardened
for show and not for use, because
there's too little room to do both. In my
small front yard, however, I've managed
to build a patio and make a welcoming landscape. I
walled in the patio without making a fortress that would
shun the neighborhood. Windows in the wall, a broad
path to the front gate, and perennial flowers make the
front yard inviting. Hidden behind the wall, a fountain
and intimate plantings offer a cool refuge.

When my wife, Jan, and I went looking for a larger
home back in 1987, this one looked lackluster from the
street. But we liked the neighborhood, the interior was
perfect, and we decided we could remedy the facade with
landscaping.

Shortly after we moved in, I began playing with the
50-by-100-foot lot on paper. Since we enjoy having meals

outdoors, we wanted some part of the property devoted to an area for sitting and relaxing. And since we planned to eventually add on to the house in the back, it seemed best to create a private area in front. Also, despite the street noise, the front yard is more pleasant than the back in the heat of the day because it faces north. In our previous house, we had built a partially fenced courtyard and entry that featured a fish pond, waterfall, and some lush landscaping. I decided to do something similar here.

WATER AND STONEWORK

There were two elements I wanted to incorporate in the design: stone and the sound of water. In my work as a landscape architect, I have come to view the sound of water as a necessity. It adds a note of serenity that's difficult to duplicate any other way, while masking intrusive noises from the street. Stone is a common building material in our neighborhood. The local building stone—called engineer's rock—has attractive light earth tones and grays, and it's plentiful and relatively inexpensive.

A narrow pool runs along the front wall, and plants in pots provide accents of color. The twisting-steel gate was a gift made by the author's boss, Jack Chandler, a sculptor and landscape architect.

"I have come to view the sound of water as a necessity. It adds a note of serenity that's difficult to duplicate any other way, while masking intrusive noises from the street."

I decided to build a brick patio in front of the house and surround it with a stone wall. The brick from the existing steps to the house inspired the choice of paving. The wall layout was dictated by the 20-foot setback required by the city. Because the street runs at an angle to the house, I had to jog the wall (see the site plan at right).

I wanted a wall, but I didn't want a fortress. I included three features that seem to shrink the mass of stone: I set the height at 5 feet (without sacrificing privacy), I incorporated three grid-filled windows, and then, on the street side, I designed a planter with a knee-high stone wall on three sides. Because it steps down to the low wall, the high wall seems less massive. Crape myrtles in the 18-inch high planter also make the front yard more neighborly; they offer interesting bark in winter and white flowers in summer.

I decided to install a narrow reflecting pool and fountain along the inside of the front wall. The location makes the fountain visible from the house, and the long, narrow shape of the reflecting pool minimizes the area it takes from the patio and maximizes the sound of the falling water. Three concrete lions' heads set into the wall jet water into the pool.

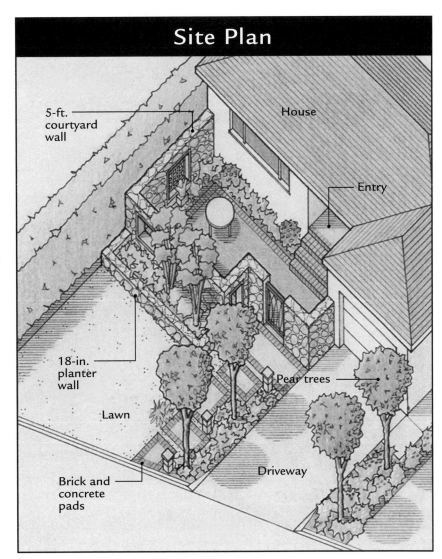

Site Plan

5-ft. courtyard wall

House

Entry

18-in. planter wall

Pear trees

Lawn

Brick and concrete pads

Driveway

> *"Pedestrians should be given their own path, instead of having to walk on the driveway to get to the front door."*

A wooden lighting fixture designed by the author's company illuminates the walk to the courtyard. By alternating the paving rectangles crosswise and lengthwise and leaving gaps between them, the author created spaces for plantings.

LIGHTS

Lighting also played a key role in the design. I'd never used low-voltage lights before, so I was anxious to experiment with some of the newer products on the market. While low-voltage lights, in my experience, have limitations in large projects, for a project of this size, they work beautifully. These lights are simple to install, don't require an electrician, and the cable can be buried, instead of being installed in conduit.

Many people are familiar with the mushroom lights found in hardware stores, but there are more options available. It takes a little research at a good lighting showroom to discover the wide range of fixtures for low-voltage systems, but it's time well spent.

I chose canisters that shine upward, concealed in the raised planter, to highlight the crape myrtles and illuminate the outside of the wall for street-side viewing. Inside the courtyard, I placed a floodlight on the wall, a narrow-focus spotlight on a garden statue, and a special underwater unit in the fountain. I also used custom wood garden lights of our firm's design along the entry path.

THE ENTRY PATH

The final element of the design was the path from the courtyard to the street. I feel strongly that pedestrians should be given their own path, instead of having to walk on the driveway to get to the front door. I decided to remove half the driveway to make room for the path and for more plants.

I designed a series of concrete rectangles edged with the same brick used in the patio

(ABOVE) A raised planter filled with crape myrtles makes the stone wall around the courtyard in front of the house seem less imposing and more neighborly. A window and an airy gate also lessen the mass of the wall. Concrete ducks and a collection of potted plants greet visitors.

(LEFT) Colorful Iceland poppies in pots brighten corners of the court-yard, adding to the limited planting spaces around two sides of the patio.

Project Construction

My wife and I did virtually all the construction. We started by saw-cutting and removing half the driveway and digging the retaining wall footings. We broke the concrete driveway remnants into chunks and recycled them into the 1-foot footings for the wall. I put steel in the footings and pre-plumbed the electrical, irrigation, and fountain systems before the start of wall construction.

The stone we used was left over from a job our firm had previously completed, and I borrowed a truck, hauled the stone over, and dumped it in the front yard. I also constructed the wooden grid "windows" so they could be installed as the walls went up.

I hired a crew of masons to build the wall because I felt uncomfortable attempting it myself. They started laying up rock under my direction, and I worked with them to safeguard all the plumbing and to ensure that the windows went in according to plan. As the walls reached toward 5 feet, I sensed that many of the neighbors had some serious reservations about the design and were wondering just what these new folks on the block might be up to.

Once the walls were completed, we excavated soil from the courtyard for the reflecting pool. Because I wanted the trough to be outfitted with ball valves, suction, overflow, and drain to control water flow through the lions' heads, I knew I couldn't use a plastic liner. Concrete was too expensive, so I decided to use fiberglass. I built a frame of pressure-treated lumber, then fiberglassed over it and painted the surface black. I had never worked with fiberglass before, but found it an easy material to use.

A filter and pump for the fountain came from a pool contractor friend who had removed them from a pool that was being upgraded. I installed the pump around the corner of the house, so its hum does not mask the sound of water from the fountain.

Once the pool was in place, we poured a concrete slab in the courtyard. Then we laid a course of bricks around the slab and filled in with bricks laid butt-to-butt on a ½-inch mortar setting bed.

The pads for the path are 4 inches deep, reinforced with wire mesh. I made the wood forms so the concrete had a ledge around the perimeter for the brick edging.

for the path. I placed the rectangles alternately crosswise and lengthwise to create planting spaces and keep the path from marching parallel with the driveway. A ground cover of blue star creeper (*Laurentia fluviatilis*, sometimes listed as *Isotoma fluviatilis*), fills the 6-inch spaces between the pads. Other perennials and ornamental grasses provide additional color and foliage texture. The wooden lights illuminate them at night.

I never drew up a formal planting plan. Instead, I located sites for trees, lawn area, and shrub beds, and selected plants later, at planting time, based on their availability and how they suited the landscape.

PLANTING

After we finished the wall, path, and patio, we turned to the irrigation and electrical systems, and finally to planting. I dug sprinkler trenches, laid pipes and wiring, and installed sprinkler heads and lights. We amended the soil in the lawn area and laid down sod. Then I planted the rest of the yard in perennials. We wanted to have color for as much of the year as possible, but the available planting areas are small and narrow, so I chose small or dwarf cultivars. We also added spring-flowering bulbs to replace those torn up in construction.

It wasn't until the garden was planted that our neighbors began to admit their initial hesitations about the design. I think many had been afraid that we were walling them out rather than creating a more pleasing environment for all. The courtyard's northerly orientation makes it a wonderful place to eat lunch or dinner on a hot summer's day. The sound of water draws us to the courtyard almost daily. And the neighbors have adopted our yard for visiting, playing, and relaxing.

GEORGE RADFORD

is a lifelong horticulturist who now gardens at home and as a volunteer at Government House in Victoria, British Columbia.

Extend Your Living Space with a
Patio Garden

Enclosing a garden can make it intimate and inviting. A trellis-work screen supports climbing vines and separates the patio from the author's back garden.

H IGH IN AN OLD hawthorn tree, a purple finch sings. Soon he flies down to drink from a small pond a few feet away from my wicker chair. Then he darts back to his nest. My portly, old cat pads his way onto the patio and stretches out at my feet in the sun. We are at peace in our paradise.

My chair sits where I used to park my car. After moving to this home in Victoria several years ago, I missed our former home's sheltered verandah. My partner, Bruce Gibson-Bean, and I realized we needed an outside living room, a place to relax, entertain, write letters, or simply gaze at our plants. So we turned our horseshoe-shaped driveway and the area surrounding it into a lush patio garden. It's now one of the most inviting spots on our property.

DEFINE THE SPACE
AND MAKE IT COZY

There are many ways to fashion an outdoor living space. If you don't have a terrace or patio, evaluate the potential for using a flat surface, such as a driveway or level lawn area. Initially, you can just set up a few chairs and tables and see how the space feels, as we did with our driveway. Then you can decide if you want to install some type of floor surface, such as brick, flagstone, or interlocking pavers.

Since we wanted to keep using the area next to the garage (which is where we over-winter potted plants) for repotting and other garden projects, we decided to keep the blacktop surface as our patio floor. We saved money, and the asphalt has been easy to maintain. It doesn't hold much heat since there's actually very little of it exposed to bright sun.

To provide privacy, shade, and shelter from wind and other elements, I think it's always good to create an enclosure around a

Foster unity in a patio setting by repeating colors and textures. All wooden structures in this garden were stained dark brown. The empty pots tucked in this trellis in a decorative pattern tie in with terra-cotta containers holding plantings here and throughout the garden.

patio garden. Often you can rely on existing walls, hedges, or other plantings as a starting point. For example, we used a cypress hedge along the property line as one border for our patio and a wall of our house as another. A pair of golden chain trees (*Laburnum* × *watereri* 'Vossii') and a low cypress hedge bordering the front of the property formed part of a third wall.

Structures such as arbors, trellises, and fencing can also provide enclosure. To separate our patio from our back garden and to disguise the area in front of the garage, we built a series of trelliswork screens. We use these trellises to support climbing plants and to hold empty terra-cotta pots placed as decorative elements. We also built fence panels and wooden gates to screen the front border of the patio.

SHADE SEATING AREAS

To make a patio an attractive extension of your home, it must be cozy. Whether you set up a table and chairs for dining, or simply include casual seating in one or more groupings, make sure your furnishings are comfortable and able to withstand your weather.

Within the courtyard we created—a space about 30 by 30 feet—we designated an area under the shade of an old plum tree for seating. It's furnished with old wicker chairs with cushions that can tolerate outdoor conditions, although we bring the cushions in when rain is forecast.

To enhance a patio's comfort, also address practical issues such as shielding traffic and other noise, harsh sunlight, and wind. Our mature trees and trellis structures provide shade and shelter from strong winds. We also have an umbrella in a stand that creates extra shade if we need it. And the sound of water softly falling from our fountain into the

These wicker chairs, shaded by an old plum tree, are well used in this outdoor living room, which was fashioned from a horseshoe-shaped driveway.

> *"Ideally, a patio garden should have at least one framed view to enjoy."*

PLACE A PATIO TO ENJOY FRAMED VIEWS

Ideally, a patio garden should have at least one framed view to enjoy. For example, a sitting area can overlook a pond, a perennial border, a raised bed of annuals, a specimen tree, or a fixed focal point like a statue. Our sitting area faces a small water garden we built where formerly there was lawn. Beyond that, we view the trellis screen, which spills over with lush-leaved plants. An elegant wrought-iron gate in the trellis wall beckons us to the garden beyond.

pond deadens any traffic noise and sometimes induces a snooze.

If your seating area is short on shade, consider installing a pergola, shade tree, or some type of awning. Creating a covered structure over part of a patio will give you more protection from the elements and enable you to leave upholstered furniture outside.

Create at least one focal point for a patio. Cherubs emerging from within a planting of purple sage (*Salvia officinalis* 'Purpurascens') subtly draw attention.

We created another focal point against the backdrop of part of the trellis screen, a section that shields the garage from view. As we enter our courtyard, we're welcomed by "Flora," a 5-foot-tall, patinated, concrete statue. She rests on a pedestal, flanked by two large cabbage palms (*Cordyline australis*). The background trellis is draped with golden hops (*Humulus lupulus* 'Aureus'). From this point you may proceed along a semicircular pathway of planted containers to the seating area or continue straight ahead into the rear garden.

In the garden of our friends Jerry and Hazel Van Slyke, a circular patio made of brick faces a free-standing trellis screen that is surrounded by perennials in raised beds. Sitting on their patio, you find your eye drawn to a sunny patch of lawn and to a greenhouse filled with plants in the distance.

CREATE INTEREST WITH VINES AND POTTED PLANTS

Climbing plants quickly embellish a trellis or arbor. We planted golden honeysuckle (*Lonicera periclymenum* 'Graham Thomas') for a long flowering season and delicious scent. Winter jasmine (*Jasminum nudiflorum*) and common or florist's jasmine (*Jasminum officinale*) create a lovely background for the David Austin rose 'Golden Celebration', which is trained as a climber.

A bronze-leaved clematis (*Clematis montana* 'Elizabeth'), with its vines of deep rose flowers, lights up the lacy fingers of variegated ivies twisting their way through the woodwork. Potato vine (*Solanum jasminoides* 'Album') combines its delicate, white flowers with golden hops leaves, creating an elegant and fragrant enclosure.

I also play around with potted plantings. I especially like plants with large-leaved foliage, like *Canna*, since they give a patio an exotic flavor. With potted plants, I can easily rearrange a planting scheme. I keep a dolly on hand for this purpose.

UNIFY YOUR DESIGN ELEMENTS

To unify elements within a patio garden, it helps to choose a color palette for hardscaping and furnishings, as well as for plantings. As a background for our plantings, we chose a dark brown stain for all wooden structures, and a light gray-green paint for the wicker furniture. Deep jewel-toned chair cushions complement the plantings. We also wired small terra-cotta pots into our trelliswork

Lush container plantings add to the intimacy of a patio garden. The author grows tropical plantings along with traditional perennials and grasses in pots.

panels to personalize a common design motif and to echo the shape, color, and texture of containers on the patio floor.

Our friends the Van Slykes used a redwood stain for their wooden structures, which mellowed with exposure to sun and rain. The muted color harmonizes with their buff-colored paving, forming an earth-tone background for the foliage and flowers in terra-cotta pots. For an aged-wood look, just let cedar or redwood weather naturally. If you're considering painting structures white or a light color, keep in mind that they can draw too much attention and show dirt more easily.

There are many ways to create unity with plantings, such as repeating plants with similar colors or foliage patterns. For example, I always include several ornamental grasses like *Miscanthus* spp., spiky plants like *Cordyline* spp., and plants with variegated foliage. Many of our plantings have foliage or flowers in shades of pink, bronze, gray, and silver.

I find I never tire of spending time in our patio garden. Even watering is relaxing in such a peaceful setting. It's a meditative experience of savoring scents, sights, and birdsong in the quiet morning air.

The palette for the author's patio plantings emphasizes foliage and flowers in shades of pink, purple, bronze, silver, and gray.

JERRY GLICK

is a lifelong gardener whose garden has been featured on tours, PBS's *The Victory Garden,* and in magazines. He gardens in the historic German Village neighborhood of Columbus, Ohio.

A Cozy
Sitting Garden

A chair waits invitingly in the shade of a hawthorn tree in the author's garden. Nearby, a flower bed blazes with red nicotianas and wax begonias, yellow tuberous begonias, and coreopsis. Tall umbrella plants cool their feet in a tiny pond. (Photo taken at A on site plan.)

I FEEL THAT every garden, regardless of size, needs an intimate spot for relaxing, reading a good book, enjoying colorful flowers, or listening to the sound of water splashing in a pool. My backyard presented the perfect opportunity to make such a spot. In the Columbus, Ohio, neighborhood where I live, the 19th-century brick cottages sit close together on postage-stamp-sized lots—my backyard is just 30 by 40 feet, so I had to figure out how to fit everything I wanted in a limited area. I hoped to create a private garden getaway—a place to rest body and soul that would be loaded with annuals and perennials for season-long color.

I used several design techniques that work equally well in small or large gardens. With my approach, you could make a colorful sitting nook, a patio or deck garden, or a series of small gardens within a larger one. Here are my ideas for creating a sense of spaciousness, framing views, adding height to the garden, establishing resting places, and growing flowering plants for all-season color.

Prune trees in keeping with scale of garden.

A fence creates privacy and serves as a backdrop for plants.

Screen areas with plants to create a sense of mystery.

Choose paving materials to complement the house.

Paths give the garden a sense of order.

"Placing plants or objects so they must be walked around to see what's beyond creates mystery and suggests there is more garden just out of sight."

CREATING A SENSE OF SPACIOUSNESS

When I moved in, my tiny yard was overgrown with ivy, shrubs, and trees. I created the illusion of spaciousness by making open areas—a deck and a patio—and ringing them with flower beds. Dividing the garden into several small, distinct areas also makes it seem bigger.

In such a small garden, or in small areas within a larger garden, it is especially important to leave some space open to prevent a cluttered look and to lead the eye through the design. I cleared away all the trees except a weeping cherry, a crabapple, and a hawthorn, and I pruned them to a size in keeping with the small yard. Paths between the beds keep the plants from running together in an untidy jumble and lead people through the garden. A brick patio gives me and my guests some elbow room.

The materials I chose for paving and for a fence are unobtrusive, matching the house and a carriage house at the back of the property. The patio, which sits behind the brick house, is made of salvaged brick. A low deck of weathered wood surrounds a little pond, and a boardwalk runs along the back of the garden, blending in with the wooden fence and wood siding of the carriage house.

To increase the sense of spaciousness, I also used a few optical tricks when I laid out my garden. Placing plants or objects so they must be walked around to see what's beyond creates mystery and suggests there is more garden

just out of sight. Visitors then anticipate whatever lies on the other side. To give this impression, I surrounded the deck and patio with planting beds and paths laid out at angles that force people to walk around each one to see the next. To partially screen some areas of the garden from others, I planted tall plants such as butterfly bush (*Buddleia davidii* 'Black Knight'), a summer-blooming, woody shrub, in the beds and umbrella plant (*Cyperus alternifolius*) in the pond.

ADDING PRIVACY AND HEIGHT

I wanted a tranquil garden oasis; with neighbors on both sides, I had to make it private. So I surrounded the garden with a 6-foot-tall wooden fence. The fence effectively screens out my neighbors and frames the garden, focusing attention within. The fence is high enough to form a background for the tall plants in the garden. It's also a foil for the large hanging baskets suspended from the trees, and for half-baskets loaded with colorful annuals attached to it. The fence, tall plants, and hanging baskets all draw the eye upward, vertically increasing the apparent size of the garden.

PLACES TO REST THE BODY AND SOUL

With so many plants in a garden, the eye needs a few large, simple shapes to contemplate; the body needs a shady spot in which to sit and listen to restful sounds. My fish pond, complete with water plants and a small, cascading waterfall, is only a couple of feet in diameter—in keeping with the overall proportions of the garden—but the soothing sound of running water and the glint of goldfish beneath its surface offer immense rewards. It is situated nearly in the center of everything. Next to the pond, a white canvas chair draws me like a beacon to the shade of the hawthorn tree, where I can sit and survey the entire garden. On the patio, a white umbrella-table and chairs offer another shady spot to sit.

Site Plan

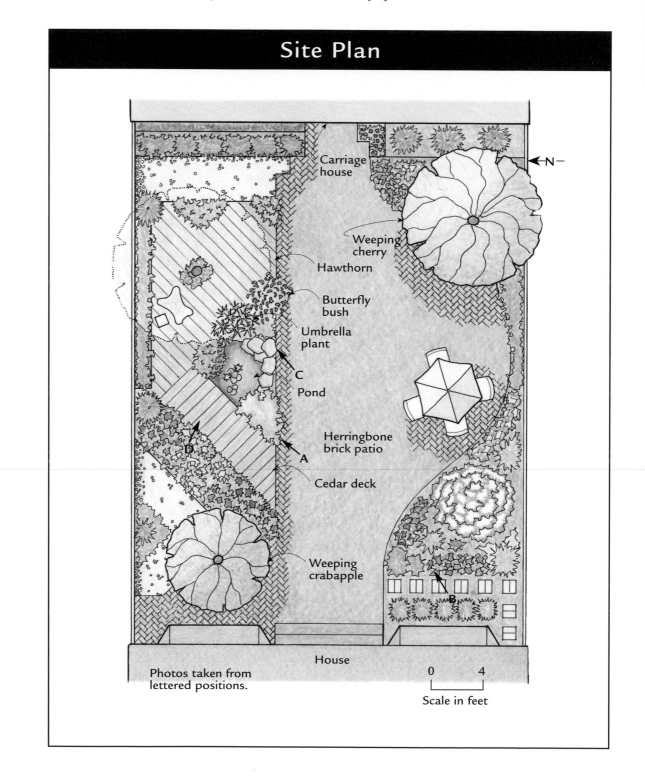

Carriage house

Weeping cherry

Hawthorn

Butterfly bush

Umbrella plant

C

Pond

Herringbone brick patio

Cedar deck

Weeping crabapple

A

D

B

N—

House

Photos taken from lettered positions.

0   4

Scale in feet

SPLASHES OF COLOR ALL SEASON

I pack my flowers together cottage-garden fashion in an exuberant mix of colors and textures that overlap and spill onto the paving. I use a combination of annuals and perennials in a variety of heights and leaf textures. My garden is small, however, so I don't have the luxury of planting indiscriminately. I select my plants for overlapping bloom periods and bright flower colors. I also use container plants in full bloom to replace bloomed-out specimens and to spike beds of ivy with color. I think it's fun to use potted plants that are not typically grown outdoors in summer in the Midwest—tropical hibiscus, oleander, and bougainvillea. They flower all summer in shades ranging from hot pink and lavender to the brightest scarlet. I overwinter these potted plants indoors.

In order to make my limited-sized garden interesting, functional, and private, I let my wishes overcome conventional wisdom, which suggests that it takes a big area to have a great garden. I say that it just takes some imagination, lots of plants, and a few design tricks. Last summer I managed to keep annuals in full color late into the season, when they join the mums in a crescendo of color.

My little garden lets me block out the hubbub of city life. Here I enter a world of nature where I watch squirrels, birds, and butterflies. Last summer I had garden visitors daily; their enjoyment plus my own was reward enough.

A hawthorn tree and a weeping cherry partially disguise the facade of an old carriage house and add vertical scale to the author's backyard sitting garden. (Photo taken at D on site plan.)

Yellow-flowered heliopsis and lavender butterfly bush tower over pink bleeding-hearts, pink begonias, yellow coreopsis, and pink verbena. (Photo taken at C on site plan.)

STEVE KIELY

is a landscape designer who enjoys his garden year-round in Denver, Colorado.

An Intimate Garden for Entertaining

Viewed from the upper deck outside the author's house, a partially enclosed dining patio in the distance beckons. Dividing the garden into separate areas provides places for relaxing alone or entertaining friends, and makes a small yard seem more spacious.

WHEN I MOVED into my 1920's cottage six years ago, it had a small, narrow backyard that overlooked the neighbors' yards and was exposed to a noisy street. The yard was a patch of broken concrete, weeds, and untrimmed shrubs and trees. Light conditions also were extreme, ranging from deep shade to searing afternoon sun.

Yet I wanted a garden here, a garden with a tranquil, intimate, and comfortable atmosphere, a place where I could be equally comfortable alone or with friends. At the same time I wanted the yard to feel more spacious than it actually was. Since my house is also small, I hoped the garden would serve as an outdoor extension of it. And the garden would have to be low maintenance—I have a full-time job, and I wanted to spend the majority of my time in the garden reading, meditating, and relaxing, not mowing, weeding, and watering. Finally, I hoped to use the garden year-round—on a clear, winter day here in Denver, Colorado, the temperature can be a balmy 60°F.

Back then I was a novice at gardening, having grown nothing more than geraniums and marigolds where I lived previously. And because this hobby was new to me, I wanted a chance to observe plants and to experiment with them. I began by growing common plants you can buy at the supermarket, and gradually introduced more unusual ones.

Today, my garden offers welcome respite from the clamor of city living. In solitude, it offers me a quiet haven; filled with friends, it encourages camaraderie. A deck and multiple levels of patios provide roomlike areas for entertaining, dining, and relaxing. An 8-foot-tall wooden fence provides privacy and security. Raised landscape-tie planting beds of various heights and shapes frame the "rooms" and display a host of small and medium-sized, easy-care plants. Clay pots teeming with flowers and vines add splashes of color throughout the garden.

CREATING AN INTIMATE AMBIENCE

The yard had a gentle slope, so I decided to carve out different levels, ultimately ending up with three patios and a deck. Each area is unique, and I gravitate from one to another, depending on the time of day and what I want to do. Sometimes I'm pulled to a part of the garden warmed by the sun; other times I'm drawn to an area bursting with flowers just because of my need to get lost among them.

"Each area is unique, and I gravitate from one to another, depending on the time of day and what I want to do."

A nook with a view

The first room in the garden is a large, raised wooden deck, 14 by 31 feet, that extends from the upper level of the house over a garage. From the deck, I can take in a grand view of almost all of the garden. A wide staircase down to the main level ties the deck in with the other patios. The centerpiece of the deck is an 8-by-9-foot gazebo made of cedar

The author enjoys his morning coffee in a gazebo on the upper deck. The awnings on the roof and walls unroll individually to protect this outdoor room from sun, wind, rain, and snow. The gazebo is ringed with potted plants such as blue agapanthus and vine maple.

lattice, just big enough to seat four people comfortably around a large coffee table. Individual awnings can be unrolled like window shades to cover the walls and roof, offering varying degrees of privacy and protection from the elements.

Merely a step out from an upstairs bedroom, the gazebo functions as a true extension of the house. In the early morning

hours, it's my favorite place to enjoy coffee and a newspaper. I love to sit in the gazebo with the roof awning shut, watching and smelling the dramatic summer storms that frequently roll in from the mountains. I also enjoy pulling back the awnings to admire colorful sunsets and starry nighttime skies.

Big barrels of shrubs and flowers surround the gazebo, making it a cozy conversation nook as well as a soothing place to be alone. Closer to the house, where the deck is partially shaded by a large chokecherry tree, I've planted mostly pastel flowers and silver-leaved plants, spiced up with the tubular, salmon flowers of *Fuchsia* 'Gardenmeister Bohnstedt', an annual that blooms all summer. In the sunnier areas around the gazebo, I like hot colors—a raucous mix of yellow, red, and bright pink zinnias, red and yellow Asiatic lilies, and yellow dahlberg daisies. For the winter interest of its branched, brown stems, I planted a lovely broom, *Cytisus scoparius* 'Moonlight'. This deciduous small shrub is dotted with buttery yellow flowers in spring.

A private cubbyhole

At the foot of the stairs leading down from the upper deck, there is a very secluded patio, just 8 by 13 feet, tucked under the chokecherry tree. I like cubbyholes like this—places where I can get lost and no one sees me. Paved with dry-laid stones I gathered from the mountains, this private patio has become my favorite place for reading and meditating.

This area is rather heavily shaded, so I planted it mainly with pastel-flowered impatiens, cascading blue and white lobelia, purple and white violets, and cool, luscious mosses. At night, the silver-edged ground cover 'White Nancy' lamium reflects moonlight and garden lights, guiding my steps and adding a luminous glow.

Just a few feet away is a four-tiered fountain. The sound of its gentle, trickling flow masks traffic noises while providing a beautiful, tranquil setting. It is amazing to sit quietly in the early morning sun and watch the birds, squirrels, and neighborhood cats that visit the fountain to drink and bathe.

An outdoor dining room

At the far end of the yard I built a 12-by-15-foot wood patio under the shade of a spruce tree, which provides protection from the weather. Landscape-tie planters on both sides of the entry create a doorway of sorts. They make the patio feel like an enclosed room; so does the tall, wooden fence on two sides. Two steps descending into the patio emphasize that it's a distinct space, as does the change in materials from the stone path leading to the patio to the stone and brick steps.

From the patio you can see the fountain and catch glimpses of the upper deck, but otherwise it's quite secluded. An umbrella-covered table and wicker chairs make this area the perfect place for evening dining. In such an intimate setting, conversation flows freely.

The landscape-tie planters surrounding the patio are 2 feet wide and range from 1 to 5 feet tall. They overflow with plants to delight the nose and palate. Fragrant night-scented stock, nicotiana, and scented geraniums perfume the air, creating a heavenly atmosphere. Interspersed among them are herbs, such as parsley, thyme, chives, and rosemary, which I pick fresh to add to meals, a simple feat that certainly impresses my guests.

To partially hide the patio from view, I made the planter on one side of the entry taller than the one on the other, and included small shrubs in it that fit the scale of the garden and add winter interest. I chose plants that stand out against snow. There's a splash of burgundy from the leaves of a dwarf Japanese barberry, a base of green from low-growing evergreens, and accents of red from a cotoneaster's berries. The hazelnut 'Harry Lauder's Walking Stick' (*Corylus avellana*

Everyday Plants

When I began this garden, I didn't know an annual from a perennial. I bought common plants from the grocery store at bargain prices, happy with the standard fare of marigolds, geraniums, and petunias. You'd be amazed at the magic you can create with ordinary plants. Most of those I started with are annuals that bloom their colorful heads off for a long time.

These plants can keep you satisfied for a long time, perhaps forever. Or, like me, you might decide to expand your repertoire. Indeed, exploring the world of plants has been the most fulfilling aspect of my garden. Now I find winners by trial and error. In fact, I feel that if I haven't killed at least 10 plants a year, I'm not pushing myself enough.

But don't think I've forgotten the grocery store plants that gave me the encouragement to garden in the first place. I still delight in buying a 59-cent pack of begonias, and the sight and smell of a petunia will always have a place in my garden.

Ordinary plants nestle together in containers to create a splash of color all summer. Mostly annuals, all are available at garden centers and grocery store nurseries.

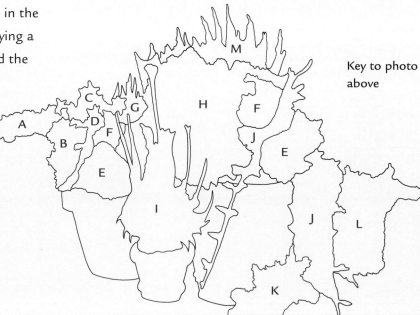

Key to photo above

A - Calendula
B - Dianthus
C - Nicotiana
D - Dusty miller
E - Lobelia
F - Perilla
G - Iris
H - Petunia
I - Curry plant
J - Vinca
K - Johnny-
jump-ups
L - Marigolds
M - Salvia

'Contorta') completes the winter picture with its gnarled, twisted branches.

In summer, miniature hollyhocks and Asiatic lilies add some height without making a dense screen. The silvery leaves of Japanese painted ferns (*Athyrium goeringianium* 'Pictum') reflect light at night, while the deep purple foliage of the perennial *Heuchera* 'Palace Purple' contrasts nicely with the white flowers of nicotiana and stock during the day.

A surprise around the corner

Hidden beneath the upper deck is a truly whimsical patio. Once a carport, this rectangular concrete slab afforded a view only of a plain fence; it was utterly barren. For fun I've recreated the panoramic view I often enjoy from a nearby city park that overlooks downtown Denver and the majestic Rocky Mountains. I built a 6-foot-wide raised bed along the length of the fence, and positioned cedar posts upright in the bed to represent

A view from the outdoor dining area takes in the stairs to the upper deck and gazebo. Small shrubs and perennials in the foreground hide the entry to a secret patio beneath the deck. Beyond the stairs lies a tiny patio shaded by a chokecherry tree.

several of the downtown skyscrapers. For the background, I made mountain peaks from strips of redwood nailed to the fence. Dwarf Alberta spruces planted in the foreground and various ground covers interspersed between the "buildings" create a parklike setting. A miniature stone pathway winds through this diorama, creating an illusion of distance. Pots filled with coleus and impatiens add color.

One of the most enjoyable aspects of this patio is that it's mostly hidden. Visitors catch only a glimpse of it through lath beneath the stairs near the chokecherry and are enticed to figure out how to enter it. From the lower dining patio, you can see only the entrance to this hidden patio, a tantalizing hint of something beyond.

MAKING A YARD SEEM BIGGER

It might sound as though I have crammed too much into a very small yard, but several techniques make the garden appear much larger than it is. Try them if you want a more spacious-looking yard.

* Creating different levels and roomlike areas encourages people to immerse themselves in each distinct environment, rather than focus on the small size of the whole yard. Even a slight change in level creates the illusion of a larger area.

* Varying the size and heights of planting beds breaks the movement of your eyes as you stop and study each bed. This adds dimension to the landscape and offers points of interest.

By building up some of the beds to eye level and planting them with small and medium-sized plants in scale with a small garden, I created the impression of a larger, more mature garden. Vines and cascading plants tumble over the edges of the beds, adding fullness without taking up much space.

* Enticing viewers with stairs and paths draws them from one area to another, encouraging full exploration of the garden and creating the impression of a larger area. But because I've used paving materials that look and feel irregular, such as the used brick and uneven stones that form my paths, visitors walk slowly and savor their surroundings. Interplanting the paving with creeping thyme, which releases wonderful scents when trod upon, causes people to linger even longer.

  Stairs and paths also leave visitors wondering what lies ahead, just out of sight. When people don't see a defined area, they often imagine a larger one. In my garden, several miniature paths meandering through the planting beds lead nowhere, but they take the eye and the mind on a journey.

* Establishing several sitting areas from which the garden can be viewed gives you a chance to see many gardens in one. No matter which direction you look, there can be something to catch your eye. My favorite location for viewing is the tiny patio beside the water fountain. From there I can see all the other areas only partially, so I'm soon up and roaming again.

KONRAD GAUDER

is a landscape designer in Berkeley, California, with over 25 years' experience designing and building gardens.

A Miniature Mountain Landscape

A miniature landscape weds this house to its site. Dwarf plants and stone raised beds extend the architecture of the author's home. Naturally small conifers and Japanese maples repeat the subtle alpine appearance of the house.

IN 1982, MY WIFE, Denise, and I moved into her childhood home. It was a run-down, Berkeley Craftsman-style house, vintage 1910. The house had been unoccupied for seven years, but it held out lots of promise. What garden there was consisted of a strip of Bermuda grass sloping to the street in front of the house. Old bottlebrush, hibiscus, and an invasive flowering quince decorated the foundation. Overgrown roses gave an unkempt appearance to the narrow strip of side yard, and in back of the house was a poorly constructed concrete-brick patio surrounded by shrubbery, a Japanese maple, and plum and mulberry trees. We kept the maple.

DESIGN GOALS

We decided to tackle the prospect of transforming the house and grounds ourselves. I had been designing and building gardens for several years, and Denise was studying to become a landscape architect. Our plan was to bring out the potential of the house by adding natural-looking redwood trim and siding, gently curved beams, and well-proportioned detailing. Once the house was completed, it inspired us to create a garden that would reflect its new, alpine, chalet-like appearance. We wanted to integrate house and yard and to get away from the flatness of the city lot. We also wanted to create a miniature landscape to fit the scale of the small property (16 by 40 feet in front and 20 by 40 feet in back). At the same time, we hoped to make the space appear larger by choosing smaller-scale features, including plant and leaf sizes. Privacy and security from a busy city street were important. We also wanted to have a view of the rear garden from the house and sitting areas or outdoor rooms from which to enjoy the garden. Finally, we wanted it all to be low maintenance.

AN ENTRY GARDEN ON A BUSY STREET

We designed a slightly formal entry garden with carefully joined stonework and neat, dwarf plants to enhance the house. The property sloped gently to the street and could have been retained with a rock garden, but too many dogs had easy access to the property for that delicate kind of garden to be safe. We decided, instead, to build low stone walls interconnecting large boulders placed along the perimeter, like precious stones in a necklace. These stone walls act as retaining walls

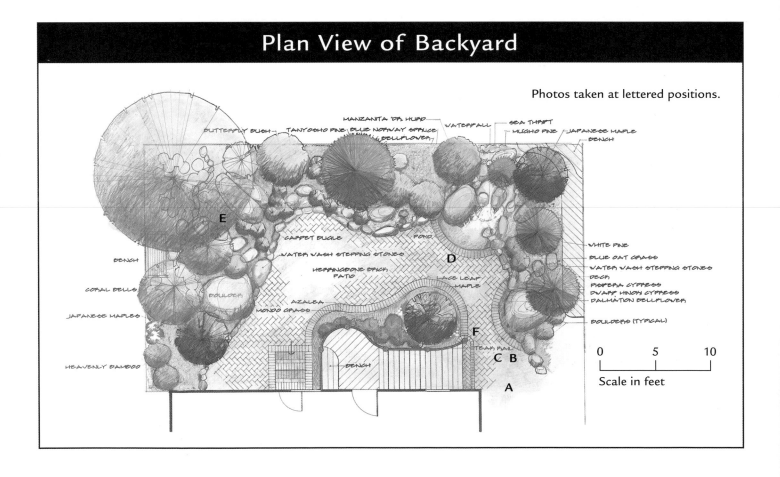

Plan View of Backyard

Photos taken at lettered positions.

BUTTERFLY BUSH
TANYOSHO PINE
MANZANITA 'DR HURD
BLUE NORWAY SPRUCE
BELLFLOWER
WATERFALL
SEA THRIFT
MUGHO PINE
JAPANESE MAPLE
BENCH

CARPET BUGLE
POND
WHITE PINE
BLUE OAT GRASS
BENCH
WATER WASH STEPPING STONES
WATER WASH STEPPING STONES
DECK
HERRINGBONE BRICK PATIO
LACE LEAF MAPLE
PISIFERA CYPRESS
DWARF HINOKI CYPRESS
CORAL BELLS
DALMATION BELLFLOWER
JAPANESE MAPLES
BOULDER
AZALEA
MONDO GRASS
BOULDERS (TYPICAL)

TEAK PAD
HEAVENLY BAMBOO
BENCH

0   5   10

Scale in feet

for two raised beds, which now flank the driveway.

We decided the naturalistic style I had developed in my practice would suit our miniature landscape perfectly and keep it from looking contrived. As part of that style, we built rock outcroppings in front and back (more than 20 tons of boulders and 10 tons of smaller rocks were used) to create structural focal points around which to plant.

In the raised beds in front, around the carefully placed boulders, we planted well-behaved, naturally dwarf trees and conifers and low plants that would hug the rocks, as in an alpine environment. These plants fit the scale of the landscape and require very little care.

Due to our closeness to a busy city street, privacy and security were also important in the front and side yards. But we also felt that openness and light were important. To meet both these needs, we settled on a gate and fence design that incorporated 2-inch spaces between vertical 2-inch-wide boards. It serves as a substantial barrier to the outside world while allowing ample light to enter.

The trellis above the entry gate has large timbers that mirror those used on the house. The sturdy proportions of the trellis give ample support to the Chinese wisteria vine (*Wisteria sinensis* 'Cookes Purple') we planted to climb upon it. We chose the wisteria for its purple color, as well as its tendency to bloom several times a year. Its moderate-sized leaves are in scale with its environment.

A fence with a locking gate provides privacy and security for the side and back yards, while the careful spacing of its posts allows light to stream through. An attached trellis supports the purple-flowering Chinese wisteria 'Cookes Purple'.

A MOUNTAINOUS VISTA IN MINIATURE

In the rear garden we wanted a full privacy barrier but didn't want to block the light there either. We chose a 6-foot-tall board-and-batten fence topped with 18 inches of diagonal lath, which raises the height of the fence without blocking light.

The original back porch was in sad condition, so we demolished it and replaced it with a curvaceous, gracefully cantilevered deck. A built-in bench on the deck provides a great vantage point from which to view the garden.

Dwarf evergreens add color and texture year-round but remain within the scale of the garden.

Ornamental grasses fill gaps between rocks and under trees.

To create a central brick patio surrounded by sloping, raised beds, we built low, concrete retaining walls around the perimeter of the property. The walls retain the raised beds and provide solid anchors for our fence posts, which we bolted to the walls on the outside. The fence totally hides the walls from our rear neighbors' view.

The boulders and retaining walls set the stage for the creation of a miniature amphitheater of planting beds, which eliminates the flatness of the city lot. By incorporating boulders, we reduced the amount of walking space, creating a sense of perspective as the eye travels micro distances. The effect is like viewing a mountain landscape in miniature.

Deciduous trees add color and contrast with the evergreens.

Careful placement of rocks and boulders creates a natural-looking pond.

Creating a Low-Maintenance Garden

We live in drought-stricken California, so we grow trees, shrubs, hardy perennials, and ground covers that do well with little water. We water only twice a week; an irrigation system makes the job easy and efficient. These same plants make for a low-maintenance garden—they require little deadheading, clipping, or dividing and no staking.

CONIFERS FOR STRUCTURE

We selected a number of dwarf conifers for the structure their foliage creates throughout the year and to give the flavor of an alpine environment. One of the more striking cultivars selected for the rear garden is the dwarf Colorado blue spruce (*Picea pungens*

'Glauca Globosa'), distinctive for its low (18- to 24-inch) growth and its fine texture, as well as its striking gray-blue color. This plant, which grows only about ½ inch per year, contrasts wonderfully with bright greens and purples and can be used alone or in drifts that mass the color for a broader effect.

A pine tree whose name describes its appearance, the multi-branched Japanese umbrella pine (*Pinus densiflora* 'Umbraculifera'), occupies center stage in the rear garden, where it shelters the patio and provides handsome structure when viewed from the porch. With an expected mature height of 12 to 15 feet, it won't dominate its limited space.

Various dwarf Hinoki cypress (*Chamaecyparis obtusa*) contribute their lush, needleless, whorled foliage in luscious colors from rich green to gold. Ranging from 2 ft. to 6 ft. in height, the cypresses offer us years of tidy, slow growth.

DECIDUOUS TREES FOR COLOR

Complementing the conifers are deciduous trees, which provide dynamic color from spring's first blush through the brilliance of autumn. The foliage of a wonderful dwarf birch (*Betula alba* 'Trost's Dwarf') arches gracefully over a large vertical boulder. The tree's delicate texture and weeping habit complement the rock and contrast with the house's natural-wood siding.

I had collected at least eight different varieties of Japanese maple (*Acer palmatum*) over the years, and I decided to place them in the planting palette. We put the larger ones next to large rocks in the backyard and nestled the smaller ones next to the brick stairway beside the entry gate to the side yard.

BROAD-LEAVED EVERGREENS

Among my favorite large shrubs is manzanita, noted for its sinewy, burgundy, smooth limbs and trunks, as well as its small, oval, gray to bright green leaves and inverted, pale pink, urnlike flowers, which appear in late January through early February here. I placed a Sonoma manzanita (*Arctostaphylos densiflora* 'Dr. Hurd'), an unusually water-tolerant cultivar with medium growth potential, in the back garden. Its position behind two closely spaced blue spruces allows the spruces' color to perfectly frame its smooth burgundy trunks and bright green foliage.

PERENNIALS

Some perennial plants, such as lavender cotton (*Santolina chamaecyparissus*), we picked for foliage color. We clip the lavender cotton and allow it to hug the rocks. Its striking gray foliage cools the eye in the bright southern exposures in which it thrives, and contrasts well with greens and purples.

Two durable, dependable, shade-tolerant, easy-maintenance, low-growing perennials—purple-flowering bellflower (*Campanula muralis*) and sea thrift (*Armeria maritima*)—add neat, self-contained foliage and wonderful flower colors that don't overwhelm the eye. The sea thrift is notable for its peak displays of pink, ball-like flowers on graceful stems. Several varieties of creeping thyme contribute their rock-embracing tendencies to the garden and provide a wonderful variety of colors—silvery gray to golden yellow foliage and white to lavender blossoms.

One of the real surprises was dwarf germander (*Teucrium chamaedrys* 'Prostratum'), whose habit of running underground without being invasive was a delightful discovery. It grows between rocks, while avoiding more open areas. This fine-textured, beautiful plant requires no clipping and, therefore, little maintenance.

Pink-flowering alpine geranium (*Erodium chamaedryoides*) and blue-flowered carpet bugleweed (*Ajuga reptans*) contribute color and durability to the shady areas. Alpine geranium blooms from spring to fall while remaining compact and noninvasive. This green-leaved bugleweed provides a bright accent among rocks and sends up 3-inch flower spikes in the spring. Its foliage forms a neat 1-inch-tall mat.

ORNAMENTAL GRASSES

To provide a vertical element and simulate the profuse growth of grasses in mountain areas, we planted ornamental grasses, most notably *Helictotrichon sempervirens*, blue fescue (*Festuca ovina* 'Glauca'), and green fescue (*F. amethystina*). We placed them next to vertical rocks, in drifts on slopes, and under taller trees.

The grasses are as easy to maintain as the rest of the garden. Both the 3-foot-tall helictotrichon and the 6- to 12-inch-tall fescues require only a trim in the late fall or early spring to rid them of dead leaves. In addition, their fine textures and handsome colors allow us to use them as interesting color accents—i.e., green fescue planted under blue spruce.

"Our plant materials suggest an alpine environment, yet maintain the scale and texture of a small garden. We chose trees and shrubs for their finely textured leaves or needles, their slow growth, and their limited mature size."

Water rushes past rocks and boulders and emerges in a small pond, creating a tranquil sound that drowns out city noise. The sword-shaped leaves of Siberian iris fan out from behind a tall boulder and provide a vertical accent. (Photo taken at D on site plan.)

Our plant materials suggest an alpine environment, yet maintain the scale and texture of a small garden. We chose trees and shrubs whose eventual size would not overwhelm and dwarf the garden, selecting them for their finely textured leaves or needles, their slow growth, and their limited mature size.

AN ALPINE WATER FEATURE

More than a year after the completion of the garden, we decided to add a water feature to the northeast corner of the rear garden. It would provide further privacy by drowning out city noises while adding the tranquil feeling of a mountain stream and a place of rest.

We created an upper falls area and small pond, a gurgling streambed, and a lower cascade with a strong, recirculating waterfall. A large boulder was imposed in the space where we intended to build the lower pond. Rather than try to move it, we incorporated it into the composition. We placed stones into a concrete shell to form the falls and beside it to frame the cascade.

The garden and its stream have been a favorite play area for our two young daughters who have grown up scampering on the rocks, splashing in the water, and spinning fantasies under the trees. In the course of routine weeding or pruning, I periodically encounter miniature kingdoms among the rocks and beneath shrubs, encampments of tiny Indians, or groups of wild tigers and bears, even giraffes and elephants, hidden in the underbrush.

Our garden has become a place of peace and repose, a resting spot where the hurried and troubled pace of life outside can be set aside and inner thoughts and dreams can be realized.

(ABOVE) An arch made of two posts, with a curved lintel on top, frames the entrance to the rear garden from the side yard. The arch stands at the far end of a path that meanders gently through the side yard. (Photo taken at A on site plan.)

(LEFT) A built-in bench on the back porch provides a vantage point from which to observe the garden. Some of the plantings were placed specifically to create a beautiful view from the porch. (Photo taken at E on site plan.)

A Courtyard Garden

JANE E. LAPPIN

designs gardens and is the author of numerous gardening articles. She owns Wainscott Farms where she grows rare and unusual plants in the East Hampton area of Long Island, New York.

A table and chairs in the center of a walled patio provide a cozy place to dine. Four L-shaped flower beds (two visible here) lend symmetry, color, and fragrance to this outdoor living area. A fountain beneath the arch of the brick wall serves as a focal point.

I F YOU OPEN YOUR MIND to the possibilities, a small space can be transformed into a unique and visually rich garden. Sometimes good things do come in small packages.

When my clients asked me to create a garden for their small courtyard, I realized I had a delightful challenge on my hands. Enclosed on three sides by the house and on the fourth by a 10-foot-tall brick wall, the site was ideal for an intimate garden and outdoor living area.

I designed a courtyard garden with principles I've found helpful for small sites. I created planting beds and a defined sitting area, balanced the garden visually, and packed it with flowers, creating a serene, cozy environment. Many of these features could be adapted to your garden as well.

PLANNING THE GARDEN

Before I design a small garden, I consider how it will be used. My clients were relaxed people with an informal lifestyle. They loved being outside with friends and relatives, and they asked me to develop the courtyard into a flower-filled haven for entertaining, sitting, and walking around. My clients also liked the prospect of a small, protected garden—it would be a pleasing contrast to the immensity of the ocean nearby.

I began by taking stock of the site. The courtyard, roughly 25 by 25 feet, was visible from many rooms in the house. I would have to make sure the garden offered attractive views from several perspectives. An existing fountain set in the wall would make a soothing sound as it trickled into a semicircular brick basin below. Beneath the tangle of overgrown plantings in the courtyard, I uncovered a path of bluestone pavers, which I decided to extend throughout the garden.

Before I settled on a final design, I discarded several options. A central sundial and beds edged with clipped hedges would look attractive from inside the house, but would be too regimented for my clients' tastes. A formal design would also restrict use of the garden to that of a passageway. I also thought about an elaborate garden of vegetables, herbs, and cutting flowers for "Dad," who loved to cook. While pretty and utilitarian, however, it wouldn't look lush enough all season.

In the end, I decided to make a garden room—an area that serves as an extension of the house. The architecture and interior of the house had an old-world flavor, so I envisioned a garden overflowing with an abundance of flowers, much like those created during the Renaissance in Italy. It should invite, even compel, people to enter, luring them in with its beauty and appealing to all of their senses. There would be no holding back here—the plantings would burst forth, unrestrained by precise border edges or overeager pruning shears. Such a design would meet my clients' needs and their

"In the end, I decided to make a garden room—an area that serves as an extension of the house."

tastes, and it would look lovely from inside as well as from outside.

A GARDEN OF MOODS

Once I've decided on an overall design for a garden, I think about how I want it to make people feel. In a small, enclosed garden, no sweeping vistas contribute to the mood, and everything has a greater impact than in a large, open area. For the courtyard, I relied on cool-colored and fragrant plants to convey a feeling of restfulness and romance.

Cool colors for a hot area

I planted flowers in shades of pink, blue, lavender, purple, or white, colors that soothe the eye and complement, rather than fight, with each other. Restricting the colors encourages the eye to rest. The result is a romantic, gentle atmosphere, even during July and August when the courtyard is sunny and hot.

Leaf color and texture also contribute to the peaceful mood. I wanted the foliage to unify the garden and to blend with the flowers, rather than become the main focus. Silver, blue, purple, and variegated leaves look restful and contrast enough with the flowers to be noticed, but not enough to stop your eye. For similar reasons, I avoided leaves with shiny textures or a stiff bearing, and relied instead on leaves with furry, pebbly, or dull surfaces. For example, I chose scented geraniums for their downy, medium green leaves; borage for its fuzzy, blue-green leaves; artemisia for its silvery, smooth leaves; and an ornamental sage for its dull purple, pebbly leaves.

Fragrance

Fragrance creates a mood of romance in the garden. It invites you to visit and linger, drawing you into the garden and then luring you from scent to scent. Each year I try different fragrant plants in the courtyard garden, but I have a few favorites. *Nicotiana* 'White Cloud', a white-flowered annual, grows to about

Cool-colored flowers lend a restful feeling to the garden. Pink-and-white verbena and magenta 'Lavender Lace' verbena sprawl over the edge of the bed. Behind them (from left to right), the purple spikes of blue salvia, white roses, and blue borage nestle together.

3 feet tall and reliably perfumes the nighttime air with heady, rich scent. For August fragrance, I plant single- and double-flowering tuberoses (*Polianthes tuberosa*). These tender bulbs bear creamy white flowers on 2-foot-tall flower spires that emerge from tall, grasslike foliage. When even the slightest breeze blows, the flowers emit a sweet, light fragrance, reminiscent of a tropical summer night. Since tuberose leaves are not beautiful

The bright pink flowers of an annual verbena spill from a pedestaled urn. Below the urn, silvery-leaved helichrysum intermingles with the soft green leaves and white flowers of a scented geranium and purple verbena.

or substantial enough to warrant a separate stand, and because the flowers bloom so late in the season, I tuck them among earlier flowering perennials. A patch of herbs—sage, basil, rosemary, tarragon, and spearmint—offers both fragrant foliage and flavors for the kitchen.

THE PLEASURES OF SYMMETRY

Symmetry in a garden pleases the eye. When I design a garden, I look first for structural symmetry—for example, paths that divide the garden into equal parts or planting beds on either side of a line of sight. But symmetry need not have crisp, geometric edges or require carefully trimmed plants; you can also create it by choosing a focal point and planting in graduated heights.

A center for the garden

I decided to center this garden around the view from the living room, with the fountain as the focal point. I planned a sitting and eating area in the middle of the courtyard surrounded by four L-shaped planting beds. Wide paths would separate these beds from narrow ones along the perimeter walls.

I couldn't make the L-shaped beds the same size because one side of the garden was shorter than the other. So, I created an appearance of symmetry by placing the beds the same distance from the fountain, by making them all the same shape, and by planting them as nearly mirror images in color, texture, and scale.

I reinforced the illusion of balance in several ways. Plants loosely spill over the edges of the beds and nestle together, which keeps your eye moving. An urn placed at the inner corner of each bed directs the eye away from

the outer corner, where the discrepancy in length would be noticeable. The urns also make the fountain look centered along the length of the wall.

Balance with heights

To emphasize the symmetry of the garden, I planted it in graduated heights. Viewed from the sitting area, the plants rise from low-growers (8 to 10 inches tall) through those that are mid-height (15 to 24 inches) to taller ones (30 to 36 inches). The layered look repeats no matter which direction you look, so the garden appears balanced. At 36 inches, the tallest plants allow a view of the fountain

beyond them and of the perennials in the perimeter beds. I wanted people to feel cuddled and slightly overwhelmed, sensations that are heightened by the tall plants.

There is much going on in the center beds, so I limited the number of varieties along the perimeter. I chose subtle contrasts in flowers and foliage, too. I relied on hearty perennials that I can trust to flower each year. Pink meadowsweet (*Filipendula purpurea* 'Elegans') bears feathery, white flowers in late June. Garden phlox (*Phlox paniculata* 'Bright Eyes'), which has clusters of pink flowers with red eyes, and 'Blue Boy' phlox, with its lavender-blue flowers, open from mid-July

Perennials in a perimeter bed gradually rise from low plants at the edge to taller ones in the background. White clary sage in the center is flanked by purple delphinium, magenta loosestrife, and maiden grass on the left, pink malva behind, and bright pink dahlias on the right.

Tall, white-throated delphiniums tower over the purple spikes of blue salvia. The salvia will continue flowering long after the delphiniums are spent, creating a long season of bloom.

"To get more flowers from the garden, I use a technique that I've dubbed 'overgrowing.' Overgrowing works well in informal gardens, where some blurring of the edges and jostling of plants is acceptable."

into August. Two loosestrifes—*Lythrum virgatum* 'Morden Pink', which has rose-pink flower spikes, and 'Purple Spires', which has purple-tinted flowers—fill in quickly without becoming invasive. (Use discretion in planting loosestrife. In some states *Lythrum salicaria*, an invasive loosestrife, and 'Morden Pink', which can become invasive if pollinated by *L. salicaria*, are illegal to grow.)

In the corners of the perimeter beds, I planted maiden grass (*Miscanthus sinensis* 'Gracillimus'), whose white plumes reach 5 feet. With its fine texture and upright arching habit, it adds a touch of gracefulness. For a fun contrast, I placed purple-black hollyhock (*Alcea rosea* 'Nigra'), which reaches 6 feet and taller, around the grasses.

OVERGROWING

To get more flowers from the garden, I use a technique that I've dubbed "overgrowing." I plant next to each other two different plants with slightly overlapping bloom times (or nearly so). The earlier-blooming plant dominates the space first. After it flowers, I let it die back naturally or prune it back enough to give more room to its neighbor, which then becomes the focus of attention. I give the later blooming plant a light feeding once the early bloomer is spent. The plants don't have to physically grow over each other, but in some cases they do. Overgrowing works well in informal gardens, where some blurring of the edges and jostling of plants is acceptable.

Overgrowing can involve any combination of annuals, perennials, and biennials. I choose plants that will not crowd, choke, or invade their neighbors. The later blooming plant generally is one that grows slowly in the beginning of the season. For example, I plant delphiniums, which grow fast in spring and flower in June, with blue salvia (*Salvia farinacea* 'Victoria') and purple and pink verbenas. The salvia and the verbenas start slowly and flower after the delphiniums, usually from late June to frost. If I prune the delphiniums hard after they flower, they rebloom later in the season.

I also pair catmint (*Nepeta mussinii*) with *Verbena* 'Cleopatra Pink' and with 'Polaris', a cultivar of lilac verbena (*Verbena rigida*). The catmint, a low-growing perennial with gray-green leaves and lavender-blue flowers, blooms through early summer. Then the verbena has center stage, blooming from late July until frost.

Borage, a self-seeding annual whose dusty blue, star-shaped flowers open in June through late July, is overgrown by dahlias, which bloom from July through August. Borage in full bloom requires plenty of room, but when it's finished, I just prune its foliage way back and let the dahlias take over.

I encourage you to experiment with overgrowing. It takes a bit of know-how and labor, but it's worth the effort and is lots of fun. The garden always appears to be in full bloom. And the plants support each other, so those that ordinarily would require staking need very little.

A Classic Courtyard

MARILYN K. JOHNSTON

Having finished renovating their San Francisco Victorian, Marilyn and Steve, her husband, are now restoring a 17th-century stone farmhouse in Tuscany.

A modern version of an Italian Renaissance courtyard, the author's garden includes traditional elements like geometric beds, paths, and a fountain in the center. (Photo taken at A on site plan.)

WHEN MY HUSBAND, Steve, and I got married, we quit our jobs, sold everything, and bought one-way tickets to Europe. We traveled for 18 months, residing for eight of them in Pavia, a small, medieval town in Italy, halfway between Milan and Genoa.

Near Pavia is Montalto Pavese, a 16th-century castle that has never left our memories. The castle has a formal garden made of clipped hedges, gravel paths, and a topiary overlooking the Po River Valley and the Ligurian Apennines beyond. It is one of the most peaceful places I have ever been. When Steve and I returned to San Francisco and had the opportunity to create our own garden, there was never any doubt about what we would do: We would make a formal Italian Renaissance garden,

filled with plants native to both Northern Italy and Northern California, to remind us of this magical place.

Our house in San Francisco is an 1883 Victorian. When we moved in nearly four years ago, the backyard was truly a blank slate. Behind the two-story, fully detached house, there was nothing but 1,500 square feet of concrete paving, a three-car garage, and a tumble-down fence. There was not one square inch of dirt in which to plant. Although we were initially disappointed, we found that the lack of landscaping gave us the freedom to create our own garden.

ELEMENTS OF A FORMAL GARDEN

Our Italian Renaissance garden has certain typical formal elements, which include an orchard of espaliered fruit trees, geometric planting beds called parterres, fountains, and an untamed area, or bosco. Important concepts in the garden are the axial relationships accomplished by parterres, paths, and level changes that are apparent when the garden is seen from above.

My husband and I felt we could include all of these elements in our garden, given the space we had to work with and our temperate microclimate. The backyard faces east and is protected from the prevailing westerly

Designing the Garden

We thought about how we wanted to use the garden and decided we needed a deck large enough for two chaise longues; a table and four chairs; a fountain to muffle city noises; and paths where friends could stroll. We also needed to enclose the yard with a new fence because we planned to demolish the garage and preexisting fence on our property line.

After making a scaled drawing of the lot, we found that we had about 1,000 square feet left for our garden.

We then looked in books and magazines for design inspiration. The most helpful resource was Roy Strong's *Creating Formal Gardens* (Little, Brown, 1989). Steve and I each made sketches of various garden plans. We critiqued each other's schemes and settled on a favorite: a palm tree in the sunniest corner; a pair of espaliered fruit trees and climbing roses along the new fence; an elevated deck with one long step to sit on; an open area for sunning; a trellised area for dining; and a geometric arrangement of parterres. The parterres would be separated by paths intersecting in a circle with a fountain at the center.

On Mother's Day, we invited two friends to brunch and asked them to help us refine our design. April Phillips, a design associate at a local landscape architecture and planning firm, and Kimberlee Stryker, a landscape architect, both found the plan strong but too rigid and serious.

By the end of the afternoon, April and Kim had nearly a dozen sketches for us to consider. The design we ultimately chose was the closest to our original scheme but with some terrific improvements. April turned our parterres and paths on the diagonal and made one pair of parterres larger than the other. She also indicated placement of a tree in each of the large parterres. Kim added the missing element to our garden, the bosco, by introducing a fern grotto in the corner. Suddenly everything worked. We were now ready to build.

Balancing formality with wildness, the bosco, or untamed area, is filled with ferns, cymbidium orchids, and a saucer magnolia. (Photo taken at D on site plan.)

> *"We thought that our confined 32-by-116-foot rectangular city lot was well suited to the defined edges typical of formal gardens."*

winds. The grade change from the front to the back of the house is so steep that the house is actually three stories at the back. From the rear of the house you can look down on the yard from above. The garden's geometric shapes can be appreciated from our deck off the kitchen, as well as from my husband's office on the second floor. We thought that our confined 32-by-116-foot rectangular city lot was well suited to the defined edges typical of formal gardens.

We live in the Mission District, the sunniest, warmest part of San Francisco. We get very little fog and are protected from the cold by the Pacific Ocean and the coastal range. Palm trees, lemon trees, geraniums, roses, fruit trees, and conifers grow side by side in the Mission District, giving it a distinctly Mediterranean feel. These similarities in climate and vegetation made us confident we could succeed in growing plants common to the Italian Riviera.

CONSTRUCTING THE GARDEN

We hired a contractor to cut out part of the concrete driveway and demolish our garage. Then we hired two men with chain saws to cut down the overgrown fence. Those were

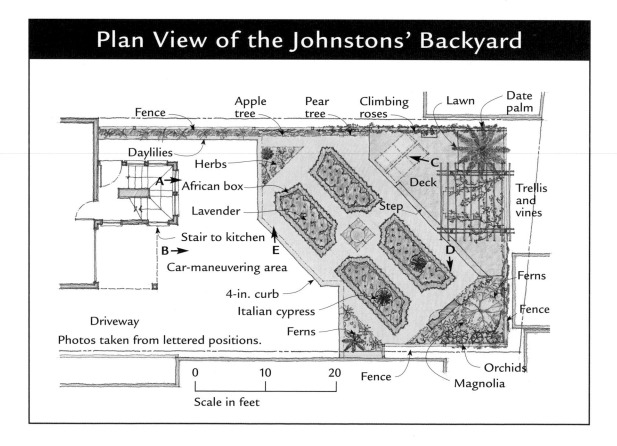

Plan View of the Johnstons' Backyard

Fence — Apple tree — Pear tree — Climbing roses — Lawn — Date palm

Daylilies
Herbs
A — African box
Lavender
Stair to kitchen
B →
Car-maneuvering area
4-in. curb
Italian cypress
Driveway
Photos taken from lettered positions.
Ferns

C
Deck
Step
E
D
Trellis and vines
Ferns
Fence
Orchids
Magnolia
Fence

0   10   20
Scale in feet

Espaliered fruit trees embrace the courtyard fence, providing all-year interest and a bounty of apples and pears in late summer and fall. (Photo taken at C on site plan.)

the only times that contractors worked on the garden. We did everything else.

We began by enclosing the garden with a new fence. All of the wood used in the garden is redwood; it isn't an Italian building material, but it is the best exterior-grade lumber available in California. We ordered the biggest date palm we could maneuver down the driveway from our next-door neighbor, Mark Green, a palm broker. Mark found us a *Phoenix dactylifera* with an 8-foot-tall trunk and a 10-foot-wide crown.

About the same time the palm was delivered, we returned from another trip to Italy with renewed enthusiasm and a plan to put lavender inside all four parterres and a pair of Italian cypress trees in the large parterres. We also decided to build two small boxes into the deck to plant with grapes.

FILLING IN WITH PLANTS

After constructing the framework of the garden, we were ready to buy the rest of our plants. We bought an espaliered Liberty

Lemons and oranges bring back Mediterranean memories for the author, who planted these trees in terracotta pots to connect the walkways to the espaliered fruit trees at the back of the garden. (Photo taken at E on site plan.)

apple and an espaliered Seckel pear, and planted them against the south-facing fence.

We purchased a matched pair of 16-foot-tall Italian cypress trees (*Cupressus sempervirens*), which we planted in the large pair of parterres. We put dark green African box (*Myrsine africana*) around the edges of the parterres with deep violet Spanish lavender (*Lavandula stoechas*) in the centers. These plants require similar soil, water, and sun conditions, and they are doing well together. In addition, like the palm, they are evergreen in our temperate region, where it rarely goes above 80°F or below 40°F, and will provide interest and texture in our garden all year-round.

CELEBRATING THE SEASONS

We chose cherry-red climbing Dortmund roses for the fence because they are disease-resistant, profuse bloomers that don't mind fog now and then. To make up for their lack of perfume, their deciduous leaves turn a lovely bronze in fall, and their spent flowers develop gorgeous persimmon hips. Contrary to popular belief, we do have seasons here. Many of our plants were chosen to emphasize those changes.

We planted 'Black Monukka' grapes in the small boxes built into the deck. Eventually, they should produce medium-sized, reddish black table grapes. Right now, however, we're more interested in the shade their leaves will provide. In the winter, when we need the heat, their bare vines will let the sun warm the deck.

Because my husband loves them, we planted hybrid daylilies (*Hemerocallis*) next to the apple tree, alternating purple 'Pandora's Box' with red 'Little Maggie'. In the triangular bed at the end of the parterres, we grew kitchen herbs. They have done a little too well, however, and we plan to replace them with roses, a traditional plant for the center of parterres.

We planted a pair of improved Meyer lemons (*Citrus meyeri*) and a Moro blood orange (*Citrus sinensis*) in three large terra-cotta pots, and strawberries beneath the espaliered fruit trees. The honeysuckle vine we cut down with the old fence has already come back. Why fight such a survivor? We're training it along the lattice on our new fence where it attracts hummingbirds.

In the bosco we planted Tasmanian tree ferns (*Dicksonia antarctica*), sword ferns (*Nephrolepis*), a saucer magnolia (*Magnolia × soulangiana*)—an impulse buy when it was beautifully in bloom—and sweet violets (*Viola*) as a ground cover underneath a stone bench.

Here, in the shadiest part of the yard, we put pale yellow cymbidium orchids that we've had for eight years. They seem to enjoy the company.

LEMON-SCENTED DAYS IN THE SUN

We finished the garden on the vernal equinox and launched it with a garden party, complete with a jazz guitar and alto-sax duo on the deck—which also makes a pretty good stage, as it turns out. Just as we'd envisioned, people sat on the long step of the deck or on the stone bench among the ferns and orchids. The day was warm and full of sun, and the garden made a wonderful place for entertaining.

Now that our work is done, we fight the good fight against aphids, powdery mildew, bitter rot, and neighborhood cats. But mostly we just lounge on our chaises and watch the sun glow on the lemons, reminding us of Italy but making us very happy to be right where we are.

Credits

The articles compiled in this book appeared in the following issues of *Fine Gardening*:

p. 6: *Clever Strategies for Designing Small Spaces* by Betty Ravenholt, issue 68. Photos by Steve Silk, © The Taunton Press, Inc., except author photo p. 7 © Reimert Ravenholt. Illustrations by Jodie Delohery, © The Taunton Press, Inc.

p. 14: *Expansive Solutions for Small Gardens* by Keith Davitt, issue 73. Photos © Steve Silk. Illustrations © Vincent Babak.

p. 25: *Reshaping Small Spaces* by Ellen Fisher, issue 55. Photos © Frank Clarkson, except author photo p. 25 © Burns Fisher. Illustrations © Vince Babak.

p. 32: *Garden Rooms* by Orene Horton, issue 28. Photos © Robert Clark. Illustrations © Vince Babak.

p. 42: *Pruning for a View* by Eleanor Thienes, issue 39. Photos © David McDonald, except author photo p. 43 © Pamela Generaux. Illustrations © Vince Babak.

p. 50: *A Courtyard Garden Makes a Private Haven* by Michael S. Schultz and Charles W. Goodman, issue 76. Photos © Allan Mandell, except author photo p. 51 © Charles W. Goodman. Illustrations © Bob La Pointe.

p. 60: *City Lot, Pastoral Paradise* by Lucy Hardiman, issue 50. Photos © Allan Mandell, except author photo p. 61 by Jennifer Benner, © The Taunton Press, Inc.

p. 67: *Hang, Stack, Trellis* by Alice S. Waegel, issue 41. Photos on pp. 67–68, and p. 70 by JeriAnn M. Geller, © The Taunton Press, Inc. Photo on p. 69 © Jerry Pavia.

p. 72: *Plants Enclose an In-Town Lot* by David Ellis, issue 82. Photos © Lee Anne White, except author photo p. 73 © David Ellis. Illustrations © Vince Babak.

p. 80: *From Tiny Yard to Private Paradise* by Verle Lessig, issue 60. Photos by Steve Silk, © The Taunton Press, Inc.

p. 88: *Front Yard Gardens Make a Strong First Impression* by Jeni Webber, issue 79. Photos © Lee Anne White. Illustrations © Jeni Webber.

p. 98: *A Front-Yard Retreat* by Chris D. Moore, issue 26. Photos by Mark Kane, © The Taunton Press, Inc., except author photo p. 99 © Jan Moore. Illustrations © Vince Babak.

p. 105: *Extend Your Living Space with a Patio Garden* by George Radford, issue 75. Photos © Paddy Wales.

p. 111: *A Cozy Sitting Garden* by Jerry Glick, issue 35. Photos © Jesse Cabungcal. Illustrations © Vince Babak.

p. 116: *An Intimate Garden for Entertaining* by Steve Kiely, issue 34. Photos on pp. 116, 119, and 122 by Nancy Beaubaire, © The Taunton Press, Inc.; p. 121 © Rob Proctor. Illustration © Grace Schaar.

p. 124: *A Miniature Mountain Landscape* by Konrad Gauder, issue 38. Photos by Nancy Beaubaire, © The Taunton Press, Inc. Illustration © Denise Gauder.

p. 134: *A Courtyard Garden* by Jane E. Lappin, issue 30. Photos by Nancy Beaubaire, © The Taunton Press, Inc., except author photo on p. 135 © Claudia Pilato Maietta.

p. 142: *A Classic Courtyard* by Marilyn K. Johnston, issue 43. Photos on pp. 142, 144 (bottom), 145, 147, 148 by Delilah Smittle, © The Taunton Press, Inc.; pp. 143 (author photo) and 144 (top) © Stephen P. Johnston. Illustration © Steve Johnston.

Front matter photo credits

p. ii: © Frank Clarkson.
p. iii: JeriAnn M. Geller, © The Taunton Press, Inc.
Contents (from left): © Jerry Pavia; Steve Silk, © The Taunton Press, Inc.; © Allan Mandell; © LeeAnne White (bottom right).
p. 2: © LeeAnne White.

Section openers photo credits

p. 4: © Frank Clarkson.
p. 5: Steve Silk, © The Taunton Press, Inc.
p. 48: © Allan Mandell.
p. 49: Steve Silk, © The Taunton Press, Inc.
p. 86: Delilah Smittle, © The Taunton Press, Inc.
p. 87: Nancy Beaubaire, © The Taunton Press, Inc.

Index